NINA GARCIA

The Scars That Save Us© 2018 by Nina Garcia

All rights reserved. No part of this book may be reproduced or transmitted in any form or by any means, electronic or mechanical, including photocopying, recording, or by any information storage and retrieval system, without permission in writing from the copyright owner.

This is a work of fiction. Names, characters, places and incidents either are the product of the author's imagination or are used fictitiously, and any resemblance to any actual persons, living or dead, events, or locales is entirely coincidental.

ISBN: 978-0-578-20911-1
This book was printed in the United States of America.

Cover Art Designed by: HotBookCovers.com

Photographer: Maritza Sanchez (lady_love_maritza@yahoo.com)
Make-Up Artist: Kiaramarie Verdejo (kverdejo96@gmail.com)

To order additional copies of this book, contact:
garciaramonita63@yahoo.com

Acknowledgments

I began writing this book in the year when my daughter Linda was born, and I finalized it in the year 2018. This book is based on a true story, an autobiography of me.

I would like to express my gratitude to my mentors Joseph Kandov, Maria Hernandez, and Kisha Morales for encouraging me to finish writing and publishing my book.

To Michael Fahey, who was very supportive physically and mentally throughout my entire career. I strongly appreciate all the patience he had for me.

Most and finally, I would like to thank my children, Luis Hoyos, Linda Hoyos, and Mason Haynes for never giving up on me, and of course, my boyfriend, Raymond Barcene, for yelling at me when I was getting discouraged.

But, of course, the ones who make a difference are my readers. So, thank you, readers, for choosing to read this book when there could've been a better one.

With lots of love,
Nina Garcia

Prologue

Why do bad things happen to good people? That's a question I've struggled with for most of my life. You see, I don't recall ever being less than a decent person. Yet, I've been through the kind of experiences that would frighten even the hardest of souls! My grandmother once told me, "Look out the window and watch your enemies pass." God bless her soul, for I'll never forget that. As they are for most people, my enemies were my experiences. Experiences that hardened, molded, and tested my will beyond all measure. Experiences that didn't just pass through but overstayed their welcome. But did all of my hellish experiences have to happen for me to become better and stronger? Was there no other way for me to get there? Surely, there must have been. I have been constantly plagued by this question for the past few decades – running around my head like a cancer growing and spreading at the speed of light, swirling with misdirected answers and outlandish outcomes. Still, this question burned inside me hotter than ever.

Why do bad things happen to good people? After thinking about it all this time, I've only been able to come up with one explanation. To put it simply, it's so they can tell stories like this one...the one I'm about to share with you.

The story of my life, with all of its unbelievable twists, turns, and extraordinary outcomes, is somehow pivotal to what has made me the woman I am today. My experiences have brought me here...to page one, where I will take you on a journey that you have likely not made before or one you know too well. It's a journey I'm still making while trying to understand how I could've gone through all I went through and survived...a journey that will surely raise more questions, such as why am I still here? Where am I going? What is my purpose? Do I have one, or do we create our purpose from our experiences? And more importantly, why did all of my trials that should've made me feel triumphant and victorious strangely end up making me feel more alone and afraid? And probably most important, do I really give a shit about any of these fucking questions? For the love of God!

Many have written stories that they claim are based on truth and their own lives. So what makes mine special, you ask? What makes my shit any more special than other sob stories that bombard us left and right? I don't claim to have had the most difficult life, and I'm sure others had it worse than me. But, regardless of other stories being better or worse, it doesn't mean mine isn't worth telling. So, even though you may have read other true stories of going to hell and back, mine also deserves to be told. Having survived my trials, I now understand that our experiences are our scars – always staying with us but all serving a purpose or a reminder. Some hurt, some bring joy, and some are invisible, tearing open into view over time. Some end up killing us, slowly and painfully, or quick and potent. But, some end up rescuing us from the abyss and saving our very lives and minds from falling to the wayside.

This story is about my scars, your scars, and anyone's scars that have given meaning to their lives and attached to them like guardian angels. Our scars offer reminders of things we needed to go through to become better people and better other people through our story – a story about the scars that end up saving us in one way or another.

Chapter 1

My memories came to me in the form of dreams, dreams that I could no longer ignore. These dreams were consistent and occurred far too often. So, I decided to have a session with them, a session where I listened to the message they were trying to send me. Once I allowed myself to get in touch with my visions, I discovered these visions were about my past.

My earliest memory is from the age of four. I remember drifting in and out of sleep while in the backseat of my parents' car. It was fascinating to me, and somewhat hypnotic, how the white lines of the road would appear and disappear. Little did I know, this road would soon become the road to a chain of unfortunate events throughout my life.

I was being driven to my cousins' house. I had never met these cousins before, but my mother told me they were really nice and that I would have a great time. My parents had made plans to go out, and since my family wanted to meet me, she embraced the opportunity. I remember waking up in front of a building, my stepdad opening the car door for me, and my mother saying, "We're here!"

As we entered the building, I became excited while thinking, *New cousins, new friends*. Like any normal four-year-old, all I wanted was someone to play with. When my aunt opened the door, her three daughters were standing right beside her. They seemed excited, too. There was Karina, who was dark-skinned and had black hair. Second was Jessie, light-skinned with dark hair. And the third was Olivia, with her light-skinned complexion and red hair, strangely enough. They were all very pretty, and I searched for some resemblance – a family bloodline recognition.

I recall them greeting me with open arms. My mother and aunt were talking by the entryway, presumably about how to take care of me and what I should eat. Once they agreed on a pick-up time, my aunt asked my cousins to take me to their room to play. My stepdad kissed me on the forehead and told me that he would not be gone long and promised to pick me up as planned. Later in life, I would find out he was not comfortable with leaving me with strangers.

Olivia grabbed my hand and whisked me away through the hallway, with Jessie and Karina following suit as they giggled at the sight of their new playmate. Once we entered the bedroom, Jessie and Karina started jumping on the bed. They invited me to join them, but I was shy. So, I just stood close by and watched them. With it being my first time meeting my relatives, I was not too comfortable yet. If my memory serves me correctly, Olivia had walked out the bedroom, leaving us to play. Being she was the oldest, she found her sisters childish. Jessie then asked me if I would like to play a game, and I nodded my head yes.

"Oh, we know a great one!" said my cousin Karina.

"We'll show you how to play, okay? First thing you have to do is stand on top of the dresser," Jessie told me, then pointed to an old wooden dresser that was behind me.

I turned to her and simply said, "Okay."

I climbed on top of the dresser and stood there waiting for further instructions.

"Okay, good. Now pull your pants down," Jessie continued.

I must have looked at her with confusion written all over my face, because she went on to say, "What? We're all girls here, silly. No need to feel uncomfortable."

"It's just that the only person that ever saw me without panties is my mama," I explained.

The Scars That Save Us

"We're cousins, and this is how we play," Jessie stated as they both smiled at me.

The warmth from their smiles made me feel safe and as if it were okay, so I did what they asked of me. I pulled my pants down. Looking at me, they told me that I had a nice butt. Then they asked me to dance for them. They started telling me that's what girls are supposed to do – dance and look sexy.

"Dance like Iris Chacon!" Jessie requested.

Iris Chacon was one of my favorite entertainers and the only person who I was allowed to watch on TV besides cartoon characters. My mother watched her show all the time and would dance around the house like Iris. It was a fun experience because my mother always asked me to join her, but I never did because again, I was very shy.

"Dance like Iris Chacon," Jessie pressed. "Let's see if you can look sexy like her."

Young and naïve, I had no idea what the word sexy meant. All I knew was that I liked the way my mother danced, so the thought of having to emulate her enticed me quite a bit. That thought made me a little more confident, and I started dancing for them the best way I knew how.

"Oh yeah, she's sexy, mami," Karina told Jessie.

"She certainly is," Jessie replied, giggling. "But, let's make her even sexier."

That's when Jessie walked over to me, grabbed my panties, and pulled them in between my butt cheeks.

"What are you doing!" I shouted.

"Don't worry, mami. This is called a thong. Every girl has one, and it makes them look way sexier," Jessie told me as Karina started laughing.

I had no idea what a thong was, but all I knew was I started to feel uncomfortable. Then, to my surprise, I felt a hand slap my butt.

"C'mon, mami, dance for us," Jessie said, slapping my butt again and again.

I felt confused and afraid at the same time because I remembered my mother telling me that if someone ever touched my private parts, they were doing something bad to me. So, I told Jessie to stop, but she didn't.

"Listen, this is what girls are supposed to do to get boys to like them! They gotta know how to move their body and be sexy, so we're trying to teach you. C'mon, keep dancing!" Jessie commanded.

She kept slapping my butt and rubbing it, ordering me to dance while Karina laughed. I screamed at her to stop, and I guess Olivia heard me because she ran into the room.

"What the hell are y'all doing?" she yelled at her sisters.

"We were just playing, that's all. Right, Karina?" Jessie stated, then turned to Karina.

Karina nodded her head nervously and replied, "Right."

Olivia clearly looked upset. "Okay, whatever you girls are doing, it stops now," barked Olivia, who then turned to me and said, "Nina, pull your panties up!"

I happily obliged. She then told us to go into the other room and watch TV with my aunt, which we did. When my mother came a little later to pick me up, she asked me why I looked sad.

"We just had a lot of fun, Mom, and I'm tired, that's all," I lied.

I got into the car as quickly as I could, and once my mother got in, we drove away. I think my mother knew something was wrong without me ever telling her what happened, because she didn't take me back there again. To this day, I haven't seen or heard from my cousins again.

Chapter 2

It was my 8th birthday, and my mother called over my relatives to celebrate. My stepdad wasn't there. When I asked my mother where he was, she said he wasn't coming back anymore. I didn't quite know what she meant, but I took it as is.

We had a barbecue, and I blew out the candles and opened a few presents. Afterwards, my mother put me to bed while some left and others stayed. The ones who stayed were in the living room watching television and gossiping. I was drifting off, so I didn't hear the door creak open. I did feel someone climb into my bed, but being half asleep, I thought I was entering a dream.

Fingers started crawling around in me like earthworms, trying to get acquainted with my private body part. Tears ran down my cheeks as I lay there. I didn't know what the fingers were trying to do, but I knew they didn't belong inside me. After a moment of vulnerability, I remembered my roots. My mother always told me that I had strong roots, that I was a Latina, which meant I was a fighter! And so my strength started to arise within me, and I turned around to fight back. That's when I saw one of the family friends, someone who I knew well. He looked at me with a guilty smile on his face, as if he knew what he was doing. His eyes apologized for it, but his hands couldn't help themselves.

As I started screaming, the earthworms wriggled their way out of me so fast, it was as if they were on fire! Then, all five of them turned me over and hit me. I felt their wrath, but remembered, as a Latina, I had my own! So, I took my finger and shoved it right in the eye of their owner.

At that point, my mother barged in to find him screaming on the floor and me screaming on the bed. My mother went over to him, and as she did, I let myself drift away again as fast as I could so I wouldn't have to see my mother inflict her wrath and to get away from the reality of what just happened.

The next day, I awoke fresh and rested. I felt as though the previous night had been just a dream, although I knew it wasn't because I still felt the presence of those earthworms that burrowed inside me the night before – as if they left a bad memory behind, a memory I couldn't shake off. It takes time.

Chapter 3

Time went by, and abuse became a regular thing for me. After the first two times, bad experiences turned into routine occurrences. I spent a lot of time with various cousins – all females and all who experimented with each other as if it was a normal part of life. I was touched by relatives left and right. It got to the point where I started to think it was normal, too. I never told my mother about any of it for fear of her reaction. Sadly, she never made me feel comfortable enough to talk to her because she was always in her own little world. I didn't get it. Why would a mother not pay attention to her child? A mother is supposed to be a protector, right? Granted, I didn't say a word, but why would I not feel comfortable talking to my own mama? Why did I feel like she wouldn't listen or that she wouldn't believe me? Is that just how mothers are? I don't know.

At that age, I was already pondering stuff about God. All heard was how people prayed for better things and better lives but rarely got them, and my mother always played favorites with my brother. She always chose to "bless" him and love him more, buying him better things and listening to him more than me. The only thing my mother seemed to care about was going out to party and having the neighbors looking out the window at her when she walked out the door, salivating like dogs! Wild dogs! That's all I saw men acting like every Saturday night as she stood outside waiting for her friends to pick her up.

Mama, you look so good! You look so pretty in your dress, with your hair done and wearing your brass earrings and glistening makeup. I want to be just like you when I grow up. These are the things

Nina Garcia

I would think to myself and sometimes say to my mother, not caring care if she listened or not but wanting her to know. Yep, it's the truth; sometimes kids don't care how bad you treat them as long as you smile at them and remind them it's still you – mama. Oh, how naïve little children are in the beginning. I'm so glad we get to grow up! But, hell, what do I know? The only thing I know for sure is the life I'm living. I forget about the kids who have it better. Those who have good mamas and good dadas, not a dada who left when they were the tender age of two. Hey, maybe that's why my mama is a little selfish. Maybe that's why I forgive her for her flaws – because I know it's hard for her. I thought about her as I fell down the stairs...

I was returning home after having gone to the grocery store. While walking through my building, I bumped into my cousin who lived there, as well. He told me to come with him, saying he wanted to show me something. After taking me to the roof, he pinned me against the door and started kissing me. I tried to push him away, but he managed to stick his hand down my pants. I froze, going back to the memory of those creepy worms. I felt imprisoned. I started clenching up in an effort to defend myself from those squirmy monsters. His other arm was holding tight, so I knew if I tried to run, I would have my head pulled from my neck. I felt truly helpless and kept thinking what to do, until I arrived at the only option I knew might help me escape. I kept forcing my mind to send a desperate cry for help, so I started praying. I prayed hard just like my grandmother taught me to do...and it worked! When my cousin looked into my eyes, he saw tears falling down my face. At that moment, I knew God had heard my prayers, because my cousin backed off me. I took the opportunity and started running.

"Don't tell anybody!" he screamed out as I ran...and tripped down the stairs.

That's when I started thinking about my mama. I kept thinking about her in front of me and asking why this was happening to me. Why couldn't she just take me away from there? I had flashes of my mama ignoring me like she had done countless other times. She looked as if she weren't here on earth but rather someplace where she didn't feel anything. I kept asking her if she was alright, but she only smiled and said nothing back.

    I woke up on the ground, right at the foot of the staircase. I didn't know if my cousin was still on the roof or not, but I didn't care. Hurt and shaken up, I walked home, leaving the groceries behind.

Chapter 4

Fast forward to years later. I was walking down the street just minding my own business and enjoying a nice day out, when I saw a guy walking in my direction. I could tell he was attracted to me; I was attracted to him, as well. Now, by all accounts, I should not have wanted to do anything with men, especially after all I had been through. However, something strange happened to me as he approached me. It was like the insecurities that I was clinging to started to wash down a little; I started feeling like more of a woman and more confident than I had felt in a long time.

Anyway, he continued walking past me. I guess so he wouldn't seem weird, shy, or both. Then, I heard someone call out, "Hey, mami," but I didn't react. Instead, I increased my pace, and after nearing the end of the block, I turned to check. Sure enough, he was gone. I sighed a little out of sadness because I didn't know if I would ever see him again. But, I was still thankful because whoever he was, he helped my mind start to feel normal again, and my body slowly started to regain trust after being abused throughout my childhood.

I enjoyed the rest of the day – more than I had other days in a very long time. I wasn't as afraid of my body like I had been for a very long time. See, I always hated my body and my appearance growing up because of everything that happened to me. I felt ugly, was shy, and lacked confidence. My mother tried to get me out of it but in her own messed up way. She would tell me to dress nice and sexy, and I would feel better and all that. But, because of the abuse I had endured, I never wanted to draw more attention to myself! I always covered myself up

Nina Garcia

when I went out, and I never put on makeup. I was ashamed and felt guilty, like my body was tainted and scarred. I didn't want to be seen by anyone. But, after the day I passed by that man, it wasn't such a conflict anymore. That confidence was intoxicating. So, whoever you are, pretty boy, thank you!

Chapter 5

That night, I was at home relaxing and reading a good book, when the phone rang. It was my friend Tania calling.

"Hey, how are you, baby?" Tania started.

"I'm good, mama. What's going on?" I replied.

"Mhmm, you definitely sound like you're good! I haven't heard you like this in days, mama," she commented.

"Yeah, I've had a good day. Took in some sunshine," I said with a smile.

"Well, check this out, mami. You're gonna get a chance to put those good vibes to use because I'm having a party at my place tonight, and it's gonna be lit!" she told me.

"Ay, mama, I don't know. I ain't into your crazy parties. You know that. Besides, I'm chillin' here at home where it's nice and quiet," I responded.

"Now, listen, don't be acting like you'd rather be in your house all by yourself tonight than with your homegirl, because I know that's not the case. Besides, it's a small party. Just some music and dancing, that's all. My boyfriend is gonna be with us, and he's bringing a really cute friend with him. We're all gonna chilling. That's all, mami. C'mon, pleaaazzzeee," Tania begged.

I sighed. Half because I knew she was right (God, I hate my house), and half because I wanted to get her off my back.

"Okay, I got you," I finally replied.

Tania gave a happy scream so loud that I instantly regretted my decision. After hanging up, I went into wardrobe and makeup mode.

Nina Garcia

A half hour later, I was at the party (which wasn't small by the way), and music was pumping through the whole place. I was in the kitchen hanging out with Tania. Her boyfriend, Miguel, was in the living room, with their friends roaming the entire house. Yep, I knew it. It was a full-on, crazy-ass party just like I figured it would be. Oh, Tania...

Anyway, I stood in the kitchen telling her about my day and the handsome stranger.

"Whaaat! Girl, you should've got his number! What's wrong with you, just walking off like that?" Tania said.

"Girl, do you have any idea how desperate it would look for me–a girl–to ask him for his number!" I told her.

"Mmmm, you got a point, mama," she replied.

"I just liked the moment, you know. I didn't care about hooking up with him or nothing. I just felt so happy as a result of what happened – his reaction to me. I started to feel like myself again, you know," I said.

"Straight up, mami, you rarely looked or sounded like you were into guys when we would hang. Damn straight took you for a lesbo. Thought about hiding my breasts after a while." Tania laughed.

"Oh my Jesus! Girl, you're too crazy for me," I said.

Then Miguel came into the kitchen. "Yo, how you girls doing over here? Y'all alright? Hey, Nina, don't be trying to switch my baby over to be a lesbo now, you hear?" he said, laughing.

"Yo, Miguel, don't be stupid," Tania fired back at him.

"I'm just playing,'" he said as he finished laughing.

I was amused because I knew Miguel was an idiot, but then I saw Miguel's friend come in right behind him after he left out, and I froze. It was the same guy who I saw on the street earlier.

"Hey, baby, you gotta get in here! I think there's a fight going on!" Miguel said, poking his head back in the kitchen.

"Oh my God, seriously? If any of you break my shit, I'm breaking your ass!" Tania quipped as she followed Miguel out.

Smiling, the guy walked over to me. I was still frozen, unable to process how I met him again, but at the party this time.

"Hi," he said calmly.

I regained myself a little and smiling back at him, I replied, "Hi."

"Didn't think I'd see you here. What a coincidence," he commented.

"Yeah, it's funny," I said, then introduced myself. "I'm Nina."

I don't know what possessed me to tell him my name first, as I'm usually shy. I guess I felt a little more confident around him.

"I'm Pito," he responded with a warm smile.

Chapter 6

People were hanging around inside and outside of the house. The music was pumping, and the lights were swirling. Tania and Miguel were probably in the bedroom, while Pito and I were outside on the porch.

"So how long have you been here?" Pito said.

"Where, in the Bronx?" I asked.

"Yep," he replied.

"Well, I've been here my whole life," I told him.

"Really! I wouldn't take you for a city girl," he said, surprised.

"Whatchu talking about?" I responded sarcastically.

Pito laughed. "I just mean that you seem more like the country type to me."

It was my turn to laugh. "Are you serious, dude? No one has ever said that to me," I replied while still laughing.

"Yeah. I mean, you seem calm, relaxed, and easygoing. Not like your friend over there with my boy. She acts like a wild party animal," he commented, giggling.

"Liiiiisten, don't be getting fresh like that, alright? Yeah, she may be crazy, but she has a big heart and is always there for me," I told him.

"Ayo, mami, I didn't mean it like that, you know. I meant no disrespect. I just mean that you can definitely tell SHE'S a city girl, but you, mami…you seem different," he said.

"Yeah, well, you don't know me. I could be some stuck-up psycho bitch, and you wouldn't even know by talking to me," I snapped.

"Ayooo, I definitely wouldn't wanna find that out." He laughed. "Yeah, you definitely seem confident like a city girl, though. Aye, but you right; I don't know you. But, I wanna get to know you," Pito said.

"Why?" I quipped.

"Ain't it obvious, mami? I dig ya," he answered.

"Really? What am I, some buried treasure? Are you an idiot?" I snapped.

"Aww, c'mon, mami. You know what I mean. You're not like any of them girls I've met before. I like you," he admitted.

"Do you really?" I asked.

"Absolutely, I do. I crazy like you," Pito stated.

Now, usually, I would've smirked in my head at his desperation, because men turn into weepy little puppies to get what they want at this stage in the conversation. Then would come the part where I would have my fun by letting Pito think he would get me and have him beg a little more. But...something happened. For some reason, I didn't smirk inside my head, and I didn't laugh at his foolish pursuit. Something about the way he said those words was different. It affected me. Something told me it was genuine, that it came from the heart.

I looked at him and frowned.

"Why you seem sad now?" he asked.

"You really do like me, don't you?" I said.

"That I do, mami, that I do. Just standing here talking with you is making my night," he said.

"Alright, look, you barely know me!" I snapped. "We barely talked tonight! How can you–"

"I know, I know," Pito said, cutting me off. "But, I mean it. I like you, and I want to get to know you, and I like the fact that I want to get to know you. I like it all! Every time I think about you, or think about having a conversation with you, or learning something new about you, I feel happy inside. Look, I'll tell you a bit about me. I grew up on the west side. I moved around a few times but always stayed in the city. My parents settled into a grocery shop. I'm an only child. I used to cut school a lot, but now, I'm trying to stop. I wanna open up an ice cream shop or something once I graduate from high school," he shared.

"An ice cream shop? Who are you, Santa Claus?" I snapped, slightly laughing.

He started laughing, too. "Nah, I just like ice cream. I don't know," he responded.

"Whatever," I said, then smirked. "I like ice cream, too, but I ain't plan to make it my life," I added, laughing again.

"Ha-ha, whatever. Look, I don't know. It might not be an ice cream store, but something like that, you know," he said.

"Actually, I don't," I quipped, then said, "I ain't ever really thought about what I wanna do."

"Well, you should. I can help you if you want," Pito offered.

"I don't know. I just…I guess I was always scared to think about my future," I admitted.

He laughed a bit. "Why are you scared?" he asked.

"I guess I felt like I wouldn't really go nowhere, like I would just stay in this deep, dark hole for the rest of my life," I said.

"Pssh, mami, you're crazy! Look, you ain't gotta ever be scared of your future, because it's yours! Your future is yours, and you can do whatever you want with it. Can't nobody tell you how your future is gonna be because you're building it, not them! You got limitless possibilities. Shit, if I were you, I'd be mad excited!" he said.

"You don't get it!" I snapped. "Sometimes it ain't that easy. Sometimes you got things blocking you."

"Yeah, but you can move those things out the way if you want to," Pito fired back. "Nothing can block you if you don't let it."

"Okay, let's just drop the topic," I quipped.

"Alright, alright, no problem. I'm just trying to put a little oomph back in your step," he told me, then laughed.

I looked at Pito and smirked.

"On the real, though, I think we should hang out. I like you, and I think you like me, too. What do you say, mami?"

I looked at him, a little annoyed but slightly taken by his boyish charm and genuine smile. I started to get that feeling again, the one he gave me the other day when I full-on desired him...and I ended up half-smiling back.

Chapter 7

And just like that, we started hanging out, talking on the phone, going to the movies, and having lunch sometimes. Pito made me laugh a lot. Mostly because he was being stupid. Maybe he was doing it on purpose to be funny.

One day, as we were walking down the street, he asked me, "Does your mom know we're hanging out?"

I was taken aback by his question.

"No, I don't think so. Why?" I asked.

"I'm just curious. I mean, I don't want you to do nothin' behind her back, you feel me?" Pito replied.

"What's it to you if she knows or not?" I questioned.

"I'd just rather it be out in the open so it can be more comfortable, you know," he said.

"I mean, I feel you, but I don't think I should tell her. I don't think she'd let me date now," I told him.

"Okay, so how about we both tell her?" he said with a smile.

OMG, I said in my head, then we set up a plan.

That night, I approached my mother so I could ease her into it before he arrived.

"Momma, I wanna tell you something," I said.

"What happened?" she asked, as if expecting something to be wrong.

"Well, there's this guy that I've been hanging out with. He's really nice, and we both like each other, but nothing's been happening so far, Momma."

I tried to be as good as I could, and God knows it was fucking hard! My mother's eyes grew wide.

"Whaaaat? Baby, you crazy! You know I ain't cool with you dating now. You ain't even fourteen yet. No way! No way en el infierno!" she started.

"Mama, I just told you nothing happened! Look, why don't you let him tell you himself, alright? He's gonna be here soon," I told her.

"Wait! Whaat? You invited him over?" she said, looking shocked.

"No, of course not. I ain't dumb, but he'll come to the apartment anyway. He thinks it's better if we're out in the open about it. I was the one who didn't care about telling you," I responded.

"Really?!"

Her tone was a little conflicted, angry about the fact that I would dare hide it from her but also impressed at Pito's honesty. The grin on her face told me that she was already being won.

About ten minutes later, he beeped me. I went to the window, and sure enough, he was there with Miguel.

"Mom, he's here!" I shouted.

My mother walked to the window, opened it, and looked out at him.

"Good evening, señora," Miguel spoke. "My name is Miguel. I think you know my mother Patricia!"

"Yeah, she's a hoe, and I don't like her. What do you want?" my mother quipped back.

Miguel gulped. "I'm here with my friend Pito. He wishes to have a word with you, señora," he said.

Pito punched him in the arm, signaling him to shut up already.

"Well, Mr. Pito is more than welcome to speak to me, but what the hell do you have to do with anything?" my mother asked.

Looking nervous, Miguel stuttered, "Well, I am here to...to...just to...uh...have his back."

"Have his back?! I'm not some mythical dragon he needs to fight! What in the hell is wrong with you?" my mother snapped back. "Oy,

The Scars That Save Us

Pito, why did you have to bring Miguel?"

Shoving Miguel aside, Pito said, "Hello, Ms. Garcia. My name is Pito, and I am very pleased to meet you. I came with the intention of informing you that I have been hanging out with your daughter and getting to know her. I really like her, and I wish to ask for your permission to continue seeing."

He actually sounded nice and proper instead of his usual street, ghetto-ish self.

"Well, I appreciate you coming forward, but why now? Why did you wait?" my mother asked.

"Forgive me, señora, but we were so caught up in the moments and laughter that it did not occur to me in the beginning. I apologize," he said.

My mother looked at him, then looked at me, and back to him. She sighed.

"Pito, I appreciate you coming to me genuinely. It's nice and honest of you. However, my daughter is still young, and I am extremely uncomfortable with her seeing or hanging out with any guy at her age. I'm sorry," my mother said bluntly.

"I understand, Ms. Garcia, but how about if we just stay friends? Would that work? She's an amazing girl, and I would love for her to be a part of my life in any way she can. Please?" he begged.

After a few seconds of thought, my mother replied, "Okay, I think that would be fine, but just as friends."

"Yes, of course. Thank you so much, Ms. Garcia," he said.

"It was nice meeting you. Have a good night," my mother told him, then closed the window.

As Miguel and Pito started walking away, Pito turned and blew me a kiss. I smiled and blew one back to him. Our plan worked.

Chapter 8

Time went on, and Pito and I got closer. Of course, my mother remained suspicious, thinking we were just friends but noticing how much time we spent together. I started to seriously like him because he was different than most of the jerks I knew around the neighborhood. I was still a little cautious, though. One, because of everything I'd been through, and two, because I'd seen this kind of scenario before where a girl falls for the guy. Then after he gets what he wants, he moves on to the next one like a lot of them do. But, you know what? After seeing so much darkness from people over the years, I was ready to let in some light. I was ready to give someone a chance to prove me wrong. Everybody deserves a chance, so let's see. My lucky chance to get closer to him came with one phone call and one really messed-up circumstance; it was a call from Puerto Rico.

My mother answered the call. Turns out my grandmother in Puerto Rico had died, and my mother didn't quite know how to handle the news. I handled it a bit better since I wasn't that close to her and had very few memories of her. I was still sad, though.

My mother had to get a ticket to go there so she could help plan the funeral and all that stuff. Not able to afford an extra ticket, she said I would have to be home alone. A few days later, she had all her stuff packed and left out the door. Part of me wished she would go and stay there, but oh well. At least, I would have the house to myself until she returned. So, I figured it would be a great opportunity to call Pito over and have some us time.

Fast forward to Pito coming through the door. I prepared some chips and dip for us, and we sat down to watch TV. It was a funny show, and we both laughed a lot.

Then he turned to me and said, "You know, I've been thinkin'. We've been with each other this whole time and have never kissed."

I turned to him, kind of half expecting this subject to pop up sometime during the evening.

"So?" I said.

"Well, have you ever had a kiss?" he inquired.

"Yeah, of course," I lied. Don't know why I felt the need to lie, but I did.

"Do you want me to kiss you?" he asked.

Now I was kind of infatuated. I mean, it takes a gentleman to ask permission to kiss when so many other guys would just go for it. I felt giddy inside because I had never experienced that kind of sweetness before. But, I decided to try and test him.

"Most guys would just grab a girl and establish their dominance."

Pito reacted by saying, "Seriously, what the hell is your problem, girl? I was trying to be respectful!" he barked. "You know what? I'm sorry, but I ain't really feelin' this no more. I think I'm just gonna go back home."

"Wait, Pito!" Starting to feel bad, I grabbed his arm to stop him from leaving. "Listen, I'm sorry, okay? It's just that I've had really bad experiences trusting people, and you're the first guy who's been nice to me. So, I got a little defensive. I'm sorry."

I don't know if it was instinct or whatever, but I pulled him in and kissed him.

"How come you lied to me, mami?" he asked, pushing me away.

"Huh?" I responded.

"You told me that you kissed before, but I can tell this was your first kiss."

I just stood there staring at him, not knowing what to say. Pito started smiling and then laughed.

"What's so funny?" I said.

"You must be really insecure to feel that you have to lie to me to make yourself look more experienced than you are, huh?"

I froze.

"Listen, you don't gotta ever lie to me, okay? You can be yourself around me, and you can be honest. I ain't ever gonna judge you, and I'll always be honest with you, too," he told me.

Still standing there frozen, I blushed but was annoyed with his charm.

"You don't know how to kiss, but it ain't no biggie. I'll show ya."

With that, he walked up, reeled me in, and we started kissing. His tongue swirled around with mine, fighting from cheek to cheek, trying to get control. It was a real turn-on...and funny.

Pito continued being tender, gentle, and loving...as I kept fighting back my paranoia. His soft tongue and gentle hands definitely helped. And it went that way all night as we got more intimate and more emotional. I finally felt like I was moving into a different phase of my life, after asking for so long to leave the old behind. Thank you, Pito, for being the man that you are.

Chapter 9

After my mother returned from dear old Puerto Rico, Pito and I kept sneaking around to be with each other. My brother was usually oblivious to everything. So, anything that happened to any of us or revolved around us was pretty much like white noise to him. Pito and I were full-blown experiencing a whirlwind romance, sleeping around and going out.

One day, my mother came home and, strangely enough, into my room. I shoved Pito under the bed so fast that I worried he might have gotten friction burn. My mother came into my room to tell me to clean up, but as she turned to leave, she noticed Pito's feet under the bed. She got scared shitless at the sight of those feet. Reaching down, my mother yanked him out from under the bed while yelling, "GET OUT!" He fled from my room with the quickness! As my mother turned to face me, my inner anger took over, and I started yelling before she even got a chance to open her mouth again.

"WHAT? WHAT DO YOU WANNA SAY TO ME? YOU WANNA TALK ABOUT WHAT? CHOICES? RESPONSIBILITY? BOYS? WELL, GUESS WHAT? TOO LITTLE TOO FUCKING LATE! Sex! Regrets! Adult shit! I've been handling all of it since I was four! I know how to take care of myself and make my choices WITHOUT YOU! And even if I need help, I wouldn't ask you because there's nothing you've done right that you can share with ME! So, yes, we're seeing each other, and yes, we're having sex! We go to movies together; we talk and laugh; and we even talk shit about you and whoever else we don't like. And whatever happens, whether we get married, I get pregnant, or whatever else goes on between us, NONE OF IT CONCERNS YOU, ALRIGHT?"

Yep, she heard it like a rallying battle cry. There was a long moment of silence between us...like REALLY long.

Then with a sigh, she calmly said, "Nina, I don't ever want you to see him again..."

I looked at her like, *Did you not hear a single word I just screamed out?*

"...unless you two get married," she finished.

I was like, "Whaaaaaaat?"

"If you really are together like that, then the two of you won't have a problem tying the knot so I won't have to worry anymore. But, if you're hesitant, that means he's not the one for you, and you need to end it. That's all I'm going to say."

She walked out, leaving me standing there shocked at her proposition. Then a big goddamn smile formed on my face.

Chapter 10

My mother went down with us to city hall and signed the document that gave us permission to get married, but we told her that we wouldn't just yet until we were absolutely sure it was for us. She was fine with our decision since she felt we were being responsible about it, and she was even okay with us moving in together with her. Pito and I lived together, loved, laughed, fought...and then I ended up getting pregnant!

Pito was happy when he heard the news but was also worried because he had recently lost his job. He worked for a printing company, which was a pretty good job, but he had an accident at work and decided he couldn't go back afterward. So, we had to think of other means over the next nine months. Pito ended the conversation by telling me that he would take care of it and for me not to worry. I knew what "taking care of it" meant where he came from. It meant he was going to spend his days on the corner, where he would sell poison to naïve souls who were looking to die slowly. I didn't approve but didn't really have a say. He said he was only going to do it until he could recover a bit financially.

Nine months passed, and I finally gave birth...and it was every bit as painful as I was told. I had my child by the bare skin of my teeth. It was a boy! I didn't even think about if I wanted a boy or girl; I was unprepared for the whole thing. Too unprepared to think anything of my baby. Just wanted to get it over with since being pregnant was such a headache. Now that he was here, I had to get used to it as I went along. Pito was also unsure of how to feel about him, but he was happy in a general sense. After all, we were both still teens, so we had to split our time between figuring out how to raise ourselves as well as a kid. Pito was out there doing his thing, while I was at home taking care of my newborn.

 We named him Jason. He was the cutest thing I had ever seen, and after a period of emotional recovery and coming to grips with the fact that I had a child, I soon realized how much I loved him. And it was kind of funny loving him as I did, because before he was born, I couldn't be more terrified. Terrified of losing my freedom, afraid I wouldn't know how to properly raise a kid, afraid of my body going through horrible changes...but what I was afraid of mostly was the unknown.

 After having been through so much already, I felt like a full-blown adult at age fourteen, but when I got pregnant, I somehow started to feel like a little girl all over again – terrified all the time, vulnerable, anxious, worried, wanting someone to hold my hand and guide me through what would be the most life-changing experience I thought I could have. However, after giving birth to my child, it's like all that worry and fear just washed away. Like my baby boy bathed me, washed me in his light and beauty, and scrubbed me with his smile and dazzling eyes. I knew this was in fact the best thing that had ever happened to my life. It's like I was born again. A proud mother, an adult, a woman. I was washed and came out clean because, at that point, my baby had saved me.

 From then on, I was always with him. Everywhere I went, everything I did, I always had him with me and never let him out of my sight. And he gave me so much joy...too much. I was obsessed with him and wasn't worried about my freedom anymore because THIS was freedom. He was freedom. Having him with me and taking care of him was, in fact, the truest freedom I had ever known up until that point because now, I really did feel like an adult. My mother couldn't tell me anything anymore. I didn't have a curfew or anything. Nobody told me what to do anymore because I was a mother now. I was my own person and could do whatever I pleased. I was finally free.

Chapter 11

So life continued in its own wishy-washy way. A relationship with my ever indifferent mother and brother, and then my surprisingly normal marriage sprinkled with moments of petty arguments. A spoon or two of happy times and laughter simultaneously filled with a whole lot of distance since Pito was always on the corner doing his thing. But, at the core of my marriage was this utterly normal thing that people call...contentment! Content with our life despite the occasional highs of joy and lows of anger, because all of these things – the relationships, the marriage, the house, the corner – were all held together by and revolved around the little bundle of heaven (James) that had been produced by me. Yes, me...the girl who grew up being touched, raped, exposed to violence and drugs, and who thought she would kill herself before she got out of school.

Then I got pregnant again! A mere six months after giving birth to my first kid, I was already set to pop out another one. Un-freaking-believable!

One day, I was in the kitchen cutting up vegetables, while my son was in his little chair in the corner. My mother walked in.

"Nina, are you home?" she called out.

"Yeah, what's up?" I replied.

My mother walked into the kitchen and asked, "Nina, do you know where Pito is right now?"

"Yeah, he's out on the corner. Where else would he be?" I said.

"Well, I have something to tell you. He isn't on no corner, honey," she told me.

"What are you talking about?" I said.

Now, the way I said those words was probably the most uncommon way anyone has ever said them. A majority of people usually say it with a certain amount of confusion, while at the same time mixing in a little foreshadow premonition as if they feel in their gut that something is wrong. So, I guess saying "what are you talking about" is their subconscious way of preparing them for what they're about to hear. But, when I said that line, it was without a hint of surprise, confusion, or anxiety. It was said cold and unemotional, because in my subconscious, I'm always prepared to get bad news or for things to go wrong as they usually do in my life.

"I just saw him with another woman, sweetie," my mother uttered.

And there it was, but I didn't feel hurt. No, something else overpowered me above the hurt. It was rage!

"Where?" I snapped.

"Honey, if you go off to confront him, I'm not watching Jason for you. I'm sorry, but I'm not going to babysit your son so you can go fight your husband and some hoe. No way," she said.

"Okay, that's fine," I said, then picked up my son as her eyes widened and stormed out the door.

Yep, with my child in my arms and another one in my belly, I was going to confront my husband.

Chapter 12

I went around looking for him with Jason, my cold heart breaking on the way. And believe me, this cold heart wasn't easy to melt! It took a lot...a warm smile, a marriage, a baby, a whole lot of charm and sweet talk. To tell you the truth, I don't even know if I did it all for love. Maybe I did it to get away from my shithole of a life, away from my mother and my brother, away from my past and my pain. Although I didn't fully believe it would work, I still decided to give it a shot. I guess I missed.

I finally came across the corner and saw Pito with another woman, walking and holding hands as they smiled at each other. I was hoping my mother was mistaken, that she just needed new glasses. But, nope. Reality welcomed me into its open arms again, with a greasy smile plastered on its cold, dark face.

I walked right up to Pito, and as he saw me coming, he turned pale as a ghost. I went right up and started smacking him. The girl who he was with started cursing at me while asking who I was and what I was doing. I spit right in her face and continued smacking him. In a cowardly move, Pito forcefully took Jason from me and started blocking himself with my son, thinking I would stop. When his new girl hit me from behind, I thought to myself, *You know what, Pito, good idea. You hold on to him for me.* I took my keys and swung them right across her face! She fell to the ground, screaming as I continued striking her. Then I went to Pito and grabbed back my son, who was now crying. As Pito started to talk, no doubt about to form some explanation for walking with his newly-scarred bitch, I slapped him one more time.

"I want nothing to do with you!" I snapped coldly and walked away, trying to calm Jason down. I was done.

Later that night, while sitting on my couch contemplating things about life, love, and relationships, I heard knocking on the door. As usual, my mother was nowhere to be found, so it fell on me to answer the door. I got up and opened it. That's when I realized I probably should've asked who it was first, because it ended up being somebody I didn't like.

"Listen, I don't care about what happened today! I don't care about the fact that you beat me and my girl up. I deserved it; *we* deserved it. I've been thinking about how much I let you down the entire day, my love. I'm not asking for your forgiveness. I just ask for a chance to explain myself. I'm begging you," said Pito.

I stared at him with a blank expression. He looked scared and nervous. The silence was long and dreadfully intense. Finally, my mouth decided to open and out came the only thing I could think to say at that moment.

"Do you love me?" I asked him.

His face went from expecting to be clocked by my fist to looking surprised.

After a pause, he answered "What?"

"It's a question. Do you?" I said.

He answered, "I do."

"I don't think you do, when you're out there cheating on me and your family," I told him. "After I walked away, I started regretting not doing more damage and sending you to the ER!" I continued.

"Yes, I know! You're right! I guess I was cheating on you! But, I don't think I deserve to die for it, baby! Look, things between us started changing, and I wasn't even sure if I wanted to be with somebody else. I was just starting to get to know her, you know. I didn't think I was doing anything wrong at the time, and then we got a little intimate. But, I wasn't expecting it to go that way. We just had this crazy connection, and then before you knew it—"

He tried to continue, but I cut him off.

"So if things changed between us, why didn't you try to fix it? Things change with people all the time, but not everyone decides to mess up. They try to figure it out," I countered.

"I did try, but it wasn't the same with us as it was back in the day. We were starting to get more distant. I was always out trying to make us that money, and the few times when I was at home, there was nothing between us, you know. You were all about our kid. We didn't talk; we barely got intimate, and—"

"And when did you try?" I yelled, cutting him off again. "Did you try to talk to me more? Did you try to have intimacy with me more? Did you try to come home more? Did you try to do anything besides bullshit right now!" I screamed, ready to smack him again.

"Look, I'm sorry, my love. I really did, but it just wasn't moving. Then I met Sabrina, and things started spiraling in a crazy loop. It was like...when I first met you." He said the last part with regret and longing.

"Okay, first off, stop calling me your love because I'm sure Sabrina takes that title now, and second, you're a total loser, Pito! A real man fights to keep a relationship working, but you never did. You just hoped it'd get better, and when it didn't, you decided to do what most men do and get some new ass that reminded you of the first one," I spat.

"Now you know that's not true, baby. You were way more than that to me," he said sympathetically.

"If I was, today wouldn't have happened, and we wouldn't be having this conversation right now," I retorted.

"Look, you never had a relationship besides me, and your mom never showed you an example of a real relationship. So now what? You think you know how they are supposed to go and who should fight for what?! Did you read the definition in a magazine or something?! I mean, people in relationships make mistakes," he started.

Nina Garcia

"You're right! All I ever knew were shitty relationships that went nowhere. I got no experience in them, and that's exactly the thing. I thought you'd be different! I thought ours would be the first we could make right together," I shot back.

His eyes soured, as he knew he was defeated.

"Goodbye, Pito. I don't want nothing to do with you no more," I said coldly.

"Okay, then. Goodbye," he tried saying with the same emotionless tone as I did, but he couldn't even come close.

He walked away, and I closed the door...and that was that.

Chapter 13

Yeah, my first experiment with love and a relationship ended with a screeching halt on this miserable road of life. When you get to a dead-end on one road,…well, there's nothing left to do but move on and start over. So, that's what I decided to do. I got back on the road of life and continued my journey! And it went smoothly for a while. Still living with my mother and brother, I kept up with school, cared for my son who was my whole world, and just took it easy while trying to repair myself and build it all back up. (What I was building back up, I have no idea.) I tried to get a little bit of a social life going again, hanging out with my girls and all, but Jason made it impossible for me. I didn't regret it, though. Taking care of him constantly was hard work, but it was also peaceful because – as sad as it sounds – it felt like he was the only person who loved me, even when I thought I didn't deserve it.

But, life went on like that, and I was content with the peace, at least for the time being. Let's not forget I was expecting another baby soon, so the peace wouldn't last for long. I really hoped my new child would be as loving and awesome as Jason, because God knows, I couldn't get enough of him. I never understood why some parents don't try harder to have a bond with their kids and make sure they know they have somebody who loves them back. I mean, a kid is a permanent contract, you know. Once you have one, it's for life! So, doesn't it make sense to try and give it your all to make that kid happy so they can return it by loving you and making you happy? Why would you have a kid and then not care (like my mother), and then live to see your kids grow up and dislike you? Like, I get it. It's tough to raise kids, but still...I don't know. I guess a lot of folks don't think about those things like I do, especially if they become parents at a young age. So, it's pretty ironic that I had my kid when I was barely past puberty, and yet, I somehow thought about all this stuff. I worried that I would probably mess up, too, but there was nothing that gave me more joy than loving my boy and having him love me back. So, it was my hope that I would have the same experience or better with my next child.

The time came for me to find out the sex of my child. It was going to be a girl. Oh Lord! Now this situation would be different. One, because I knew my girl was going to grow up to be just like me, which meant I'd have to put up with another potentially positive version of myself. And two, generally speaking, girls are far more vulnerable and likely to be taken advantage of emotionally and physically. So, having a little girl would bring about more stress than I would have hoped for. Then again, if my daughter turned out to be anything like me, she would be as tough as they come and would have a big brother to look after her. I just hoped my son didn't end up like his half-brained, street-smart, not-having-a-real-job father. Anyway, I realized one thing. Since I was in the process of breaking up with Pito, my son and daughter wouldn't have their father, and that was a problem for me. So, the time came to make a choice...and as usual, I'm pretty sure I made the right one.

I knocked on the door. Pito opened it, and I asked if I could have a word with him outside. He was surprised to see me but obliged and went out with me.

"So how have you been?" he started.

"I didn't come here for small talk, Pito. I'm not gonna tell you how I've been, and I don't care how you've been nor that skank! I only want to ask for one thing, and may God have mercy on you if you refuse!" I snapped, ignoring his look of disbelief at my coldness. "After our divorce is finalized, we're done, but I want you to do one thing before it's official. I want you to give Jessica your last name.

Only you can do it since you're the father. I want you to officially sign your last name to her, and then you can be gone," I quipped.

He looked at me for a moment, a moment that felt like forever as I saw a clash of differing emotions in his eyes. Regret, anger, pain, hate, shock, you name it.

"Be gone, huh? You make this demand of me as if I'm a dog, asking me to sign over something of myself, and then you tell me to fuck off with 'be gone'. Is that how much our life together meant to you? Am I some stranger to you? Have you been acting with me the entire time?" he barked.

"No, I haven't been acting with you, dumbass! And our history was meaningful to me until I saw you walking with another girl. Then it all disappeared. I threw it down the drain because I'm a 'keep it or leave it' kind of gal! If we split, why am I going to have lingering emotions? I'm not! That doesn't make sense! When I gave my heart to you, I was all in, but then when you tore it apart, it was all out for me! I'm not insecure with myself, so why would I allow any feelings for you to remain? Now that we're done, *we're done*! That's it! You pretty much *ARE* a stranger to me now, so what's the confusion?" I barked back.

He stared at me again in disbelief, even longer this time. Then he solemnly put his head down as if forcing acceptance into his reality, even though he wasn't ready for it. After another long pause, he spoke quietly with his head still down.

"Jessica, huh? You already picked her name out," he said with a half-smile.

I looked at him in silence.

"It's a beautiful name. That's one of the ones I was thinking of, too," he said, again half-smiling.

"So?" I quipped after another pause.

"Okay, I'll do it," he replied with regret.

"Damn right you'll do it. Shit, it's the very least you can do," I said.

"But only if I have you in my life again," he finished.

"What!" I said, shocked by his words.

"I want you back, Nina. You are the love of my life, and I want us to be together as a family. I want to be their father, not just the person who created them. And I want to remain your husband and devote my life to making you happy, not just be a past love," he voiced.

Now I was the one who stood in silence with a clash of emotions running through me, but mostly anger, hate, and shock.

"ARE YOU SHITTING ME? Please tell me you're shitting me!" I barked.

"I know how you feel, Nina. I know you're in pain, and I know I fucked up. You've been reminding me this whole damn time! I know it all! But, it doesn't have to be done. We can choose to forgive and start over. I know there's something still left in you for me. I don't buy all your bullshit 'I'm over it' attitude, and I can't imagine my life without you. So, that's my only condition. Take me back, and we can be a family again, with matching last names for everybody. If not, then I can't do it, mi amor. I'm sorry."

After he let it all out, I let loose, smacking him nice and hard across the face before leaving.

"Pito, you are dumber than I thought, buddy. I'm sorry but my child having your last name is not worth me taking you back. Nope! Not gonna happen. Now we're done."

Chapter 14

The next day, after I came home from school, I started soaking in my thoughts while tending to Jason. I don't know what annoyed me more about the conversation I had with Pito – the fact that he wanted to be with me again or that he may actually be right about me still having some leftover feelings for his ass. Quite frankly, the latter was just downright terrifying. I mean, even if I did still miss him, it didn't mean I would take him back. As I was dealing with my insecurity, I decided to seek solace in the only person I ever knew to give me advice when I needed it...my best friend, Tania!

"Hey, girl, what's good?" Tania bellowed in her usual upbeat self.

I explained to her everything. How Pito was remorseful and that he said he only did it because our relationship was getting stale, about our conversation and how he wanted me back, and the fact that I *may* have some leftover, evil little "feelings" for him. At the end of it, I could tell she was less upbeat.

"Wow, that shit is crazy! You actually smacked him?" she asked.

"Yep, nice and hard, just like I felt when I saw him with her," I replied.

"Holding hands," I heard her say.

"What?" I said.

"You saw them holding hands! And that's why you're putting yourself through all this and getting a divorce, because you saw him just freakin' holding hands with her?!" she said.

"What the hell! It isn't about that girl. That was symbolic. He was looking to find someone else! I wasn't his one and only anymore. Are you saying that wasn't enough?" I said angrily.

"Look, if every relationship broke up because the guy walked with somebody else while holding hands, then shit, I don't know any couples that would be left," she started.

"Listen, girl, if he loved me, what doubts would there be? The only reason he would start meeting up with someone else is if he either fell out of love with me or was starting to, and neither reason works for me," I told Tania.

"Not necessarily, girl. I mean, sometimes people do things in the moment, but that doesn't mean they stop loving you. Look, romantic relationships work almost the same as any other. For example, take siblings. They always fight and go at each other's throats and sometimes even threaten to kill one another. But, at the end of the day, they realize how much love they got for each other, and they forgive, right?" she stated.

"Yeah, but our relationship was falling apart before he met her, so I bet he was already starting to think about being with other girls. I doubt it was a spur-of-the-moment instinct to grab the skank's hand," I said.

"First off, you don't know that, and secondly, he realized how much he loved you and how wrong he was, right?" she asked.

"Yeah," I responded.

"Exactly! Because people don't know what they have until it's gone. It took him to fuck up to realize how much you meant to him and that he can't stand to lose you. Maybe he needed that to rekindle his love for you, you know," Tania said.

"Yeah, but I don't know what'll rekindle that love for ME," I replied sadly.

"Listen, all I know is this, you can't break up with someone after every mistake made or every fight you have. Hell, Miguel and I have been through so much worse, and we're still together!" she stated.

"Yeah, why are you two still together after everything you've been through with him?" I laughed.

"Because we never gave up. We always made a point to get back to each other because that's what love is. I thought you loved him," she pressed.

"I do! I mean, I did," I told her.

"Look, if you still love him, then don't give up over something petty like holding hands. Give it another go. Don't jump ship at the first sign of trouble. Commit to each other and put effort into not only loving each other but staying together, because God knows there's a difference," Tania snapped.

"Yeah...I just wish Pito had committed harder and didn't jump off so soon," I said with regret.

"Give him time. It's his first mistake," she said.

"Thanks, girl. You really opened my eyes a bit," I told her.

"Anytime, boo boo," Tania said. "You know I got you."

"I know," I responded, then hung up.

That night, I went over to Pito's house and had a talk with him. He was ecstatic, telling me how sorry he was and how much he loved me. We decided to give it another go and move back in together again. Life went back to pre-bullshit. Pito and I worked on our relationship, took care of Jason, and did our stuff at home and outside. At the time, I was dealing with the morning sickness of my second pregnancy. But, hey, it was better than anything I had gone through so far. So, I considered it heaven.

Chapter 15

After a good start to the second coming of my marriage, things slowly started becoming more familiar, but not in a good way. Pito was back on the corner, working long days and coming home late. School became more overwhelming as I worked towards getting my diploma. My mom was becoming more irritated and bitchy towards me and Jason, probably because she was looking after for him a lot since I was still in school, and God knows that wasn't easy. My brother was still at the same employer. I doubt he had any desire to even go to school anymore. Things were slowly but surely going back to the way they were, including my marriage. (Sigh) I tried to make it work with Pito again, but it just kept returning to the same state. Unless we stumbled onto a new predicament in life, I doubted our marriage was ever going to move past what it was.

The time came when my water broke, and I was on my way to the hospital to give birth to Jessica, with Pito driving. Then, to my shock, Jessica started coming out while we were en route! I had to literally hold her head to keep her from popping out, and I kept holding her head in until we got to the hospital. She popped right out after fifteen minutes on the delivery table. Pito was ecstatic, looking down at his baby girl with a proud look showing in his eyes. Yep, Jessica was here. I just hoped things would be better with us this time around, at the very least for her sake.

A few days after the delivery, my newborn and I were discharged. My mom was happy for us, but I could tell she was a little disgruntled at the thought of having another kid to look after. Nevertheless, she took a shine to her little granddaughter, at least more than she did with me. I told her once I was done with school, I would get a part-time job so I could have more time with my babies. And life continued on...

I thought things would get better between Pito and I after Jessica was born, that our new bundle of joy would bring us closer. That wasn't the case. The first month or two, Pito came home a little earlier every day to spend more time with her, enjoying the high of having a daughter. But, after the thrill wore off, everything went back to the usual. He stayed out as late as before, even later many times. I was losing my mind juggling two kids on top of going to school. Jessica was a good baby, a little crankier sometimes than Jason, but she was good. Having two kids, though, made things twice as hard.

After a while, Pito and I started fighting more. Mostly because he was coming home late a lot and things grew cold and distant between us like before. Unlike before, I wanted to fight for our marriage. Before, I put all the work on him, expecting him to make our marriage better and waiting around for him to save us. That's probably why we failed the first time, because I didn't put forth any effort and just got angry when we started growing distant. With more of a handle on this whole bullshit marriage institution, I put my newfound experience to use. I actually argued with him now about how to make things better and tried to get him to see that he needed to try, too. That's probably why we became more distant and cold, because he kept getting more agitated with me. Before, I would leave him alone most of the time, with fights happening about stupid stuff rather than the actual problems in our relationship.

Finally, after a whole year of having an actual marriage, I got a phone call. My cousin, Sissy, was on the other line. She informed me that the police had Pito pinned down and told me the location.

Sure enough, when I arrived on the scene, I saw Pito being apprehended by a few policemen. My cousin, who was in the neighborhood and saw everything, met me and gave me the details of what happened. Pito and his boy had attempted to rob a business owner, but the guy had cameras everywhere. Apparently, Pito's "boss" had promoted him from selling on the corner to performing "missions". When the business owner came in, he stabbed Pito's boy. Pito rushed to his boy's defense, assaulting the business owner who had already called the cops. When the police arrived, they found a gun on Pito. So, they pinned him down to restrain him until they could get the cuffs on him.

I went up to where Pito was on the ground, cuffed and bleeding, and I yelled out his name. A cop heard me and came over. He asked me if I knew him, and I told him that Pito was the father of my kids. He took out a plastic bag with a gun inside and held it up to me.

"Have you ever seen this before?" the officer asked, holding up a plastic bag that contained a gun. "He had it on him."

"No, I haven't, sir. I've never seen him with it," I replied.

"Reaaallly? So this guy is the father of your kids. Yet, you've never seen him with this gun?" he asked snidely.

"Sir, the only gun I know him to have is the one between his legs, and trust me, it doesn't shoot blanks. I've never seen that gun or any gun like that on him. I didn't even know he owned one. Alright?" I replied politely but with a little attitude.

Agitated, the officer looked at me and then walked away.

The ambulance came and took Pito away handcuffed to the gurney. He started calling out to me that he did it for us, he did it for love. You know, the usual shit. Three days later, he was found guilty and sentenced to twenty-five years.

Oh well, another dead-end. Time to start over once again.

Chapter 16

"Happy birthday, Nina!" my girlfriends screamed as I blew out my candles.

It was my 17th birthday, and I was living with my girlfriend, Tania. We had all our friends over after I put my babies to sleep. No boys, just us girls! It had been a long damn time since I'd had a girls' night in.

See, after Pito was gone, life became a living hell for me at home. My mother became verbally abusive, more than she ever was before. That's because before, it was just me getting on her nerves. Now it was me and two kids, and no male figure around to make it easier. My brother, of course, was never around to affect any of us. Better yet, he couldn't care less what was going on at the house. On top of that, my mother felt a lot of resentment towards me because I didn't listen to her and got married young. Then my mistake ended up causing her much grief. She directed her pent-up animosity about everything towards me almost every day when I came home from school. Hell, she even hit me in front of my kids sometimes, and they wouldn't stop crying from fear. So, I decided fuck it! I dropped out of high school and decided to go straight to work so I could save up my money and get the hell out of there. I worked my ass off every single day. But, eventually, I couldn't tolerate it anymore. I packed my stuff and moved in with my best friend.

"We need music," Tania blurted out.

She went to the radio and started popping some reggae. The girls stood up and started dancing.

"Not so loud, girl. My babies are sleeping," I shouted over the beat.

We laughed, got drunk, and partied. It was probably the most normal birthday I'd ever had.

I continued working at a clothing store and saving up. At night, I had the company of my best friend to keep me sane. Some nights, I had the company of our friends, too. The perks of being single, independent ladies! Aaaah, independent...a word I never thought I would use to describe myself. Growing up the way I had, the thought of being independent was like a myth. Something to aspire to but knowing few had successfully done it, or at least not in a "good" way. Not street independence involving standing on the corner selling myself to losers or selling drugs to survive. My life turned out better than I imagined, even if it wasn't totally normal. This was my independence for now, and it was beautiful! I thought marriage would bring about the kind of independence that would set me free, but no, *this* was true independence. Marriage was just independence with handcuffs. You know, like you're on your own, but you aren't free. *This* was real independence...and for the first time, it was all mine!

One day, after getting off work, I went to pick up my kids from a preschool on Jackson Avenue like I usually did. While waiting for them to get out, I saw a bunch of truck drivers pulling up. The school was next to a moving and storage company. There was a man standing outside, waving to each truck driver as they pulled into the garage. I kept noticing the man turning to me every ten minutes or so, checking me out for a bit. He was in his early 30s, Caucasian, had dark hair, blue eyes, and was tall and good looking. I wasn't sure how I felt about getting back in the dating game, but I enjoyed the attention that white boy was giving me. After all the drivers pulled in, he turned and started walking up to me.

"Hi, I'm Derek," he said.

"Hi," I replied.

"I see you here every day picking up your kids, so I thought I'd come over and say hi."

"Really? You just thought you'd come up and say hi," I said snarky.

"Well, yeah."

"Okay, well, you said it. Now what?" I snapped.

He chuckled. "I can tell you're not easily fooled. I like that."

I smiled back.

"Well, of course, you're a very attractive woman," he continued. "So, I suppose saying hello wasn't the only thing on my mind."

"Well, I'm glad I inspired more than just a simple hello among your thoughts," I said with a hint of playful attitude.

Again, he chuckled. "Well, listen, I don't want to hold you up since your little ones are about to come out from school, but I would like to take you out to dinner sometime so we can get to know each other. How's that sound?" Derek asked.

I thought about it for a bit and was a little uneasy because he was so much older than me. I'm sure he didn't know I was barely legal. I guess since I was a mother, he figured I was older than I really was, but one dinner wouldn't be such a risky idea, right?

"Okay," I finally told him. "That sounds fine."

"Great," he said with a warm smile.

Just then, the doors blasted open, and the kids started running out. We exchanged numbers as my little nuggets ran toward me. They looked at Derek after hugging me, and he smiled back at them.

"I'll call you," he said before walking away.

I smiled and walked away with my kids.

"Who was that man, Mommy?" Jason asked.

"Just some nice man who works next door," I said.

That night, Derek called and asked me out to dinner. We went out the next day, and I actually had a great time, better than I had with a man in ages. Even though we had a huge age difference (I didn't reveal to him my age and he didn't ask), it didn't feel that way at all. It felt surprisingly comfortable and relatable. We laughed, ate good food, and talked about many different things other than what I was used to.

Nina Garcia

Derek was different; he wasn't the usual ghetto-banger. He was educated, successful, well-dressed, good looking, had great manners, was financially set, and even owned a few apartments. He seemed real nice, too.

By the time we finished dinner, I had decided to give this a shot. I figured if I dated a different type of man from a different type of background (and a different age), maybe I might actually have a different type of relationship and life. So, I agreed to go out with him again after that date.

Chapter 17

My kids were learning to read and write, and it was so cute. I had much fun practicing with them, watching them make stupid little mistakes, and answering their dumb but cute questions. They were practicing talking more, too, and were very verbal. It was a different experience actually watching them grow. Before, they were just little puffs of cuteness. Now, they were starting to form as little people and learning about things around them. I didn't just melt at the sight of their adorable eyes anymore; I would melt when they formed cute sentences, used words in hilarious ways, asked awkward questions about things they saw, made mistakes while reading, and when they misspelled words while writing in the funniest ways. When they ran up to me at the end of each school day and hugged the crap out of me to let me know I was their whole world... You guessed it. I melted. I wasn't just looking after them anymore. I was growing with them, and they were growing with me, just at a slower pace. I was actually developing a relationship with my kids now instead of just taking care of them. And my friend Tania was as crazy as ever (ha-ha) but always helpful when I needed her to be.

Derek and I started dating exclusively. He took me out to lavish restaurants and places, something I hadn't experienced before, and he introduced me to different people. We were always amongst well-off people who were living great or flat-out rich. It wasn't my type of crowd, but it was damn refreshing.

Derek and I had awesome chemistry. I still wasn't talking to my mother, though, and didn't have any intention on doing so any time soon. And my brother? Well, let's just say the only way he would bother with me is if I would come to him with a DNA test that proved I wasn't related to him. Horrible, right?

Nothing crazy happened to me for a long time. My new life was surprisingly calm and normal. But I guess a new beginning always starts out good, doesn't it? Yep, I expected hell to come again sooner or later as it usually did, but for the time being, I just enjoyed the moment I was having with my kids and Derek.

Things with Derek were going pretty well and for longer than I thought it would. There were no signs of trouble, but of course, no relationship can last without a fight sooner or later. We started getting into little arguments, mostly because of the people we usually hung around. I complained to him that they were too uptight, and I kinda felt like they were looking down on me. He thought I was overreacting.

Derek hadn't met my kids yet, and if that time ever came, he would be the first guy to come into their lives after their father. I wasn't prepared for that transition, and I knew my kids probably wouldn't be either for a while. So, I took it slow with him. Then, I found out I got pregnant by him! Now I had no choice but to introduce him to my kids soon since they might be getting a new sibling from him. But, after giving it some thought, I decided I wouldn't have his kid. I would get an abortion. I just wasn't ready to take things to the next level with him and introduce him to my children. I wasn't even sure I would tell him.

One day, we got into a pretty nasty fight, and he actually yelled at me, which was far from his contained self. I guessed I would start seeing more of his true colors, which made me even more okay with my decision not to have his child.

The next day, he called and apologized to me. He asked if I could come and see him so he could make it up to me, and I did. I didn't know it at the time, but apparently, Derek was the guy who Pito robbed that night he was arrested. He owned a moving and storage company, and Derek was just going out with me to get revenge on Pito. Derek was well connected, so he probably did his research and found out that I was Pito's ex-wife, as well as where I worked and where I picked up my kids. I found all this out later, of course, but while walking to the building of his suite, I kept thinking about whether this would be the time to tell him that I planned to abort his kid.

I went up to his condominium. The door was unlocked, so I entered his fancy abode.

When I called out his name, he yelled back, "Hey, honey, come in!"

I walked in further and saw him sitting down. He stood when he saw me.

"Hey, baby," Derek said as he walked over to give me a kiss and hug. "Come sit down. I want to talk," he told me.

I sat down opposite him.

"Is everything okay with you?" he asked.

"Yes, I'm fine," I replied, half lying.

I started to feel uneasy, curious to know what this was all about.

"Again, I'm sorry about the argument the other day," he continued.

"Don't worry about it," I replied.

Alright, now I was really feeling uncomfortable. I definitely felt something was wrong.

"Okay, great. Now I want to ask you something," he said innocently. "And I want you to answer me honestly."

"Alright, sure," I said.

He put his head down. After a few seconds, he looked up at me and had a weird smile on his face. Then he got up, walked over to me, and asked, "Are you pregnant?"

I was in shock but tried my best to keep a poker face.

"No," I responded, not wanting him to know yet.

"See now, why are you lying to me? Didn't I tell you to be honest?" he said scathingly.

His face was different now; it was serious, dark, and haunting almost.

"I'm not lying. I really have no idea what–"

"Stop! I know you're pregnant. Just stop."

I was shocked. I had no idea how he knew. But, again, like I said, he was well connected. Probably better connected than I realized.

"Come with me," Derek said, then started walking to the bedroom.

Even though I was a little scared, I followed him as not to make the situation worse. Once we were in the bedroom, he walked to his nightstand, opened the drawer, and pulled out a gun. Scared shitless, I stood there frozen as he started waving the gun at me.

"Have you ever seen a gun like this?" he asked.

"No," I said, my voice shaking. "Why are you showing it to me?"

He started coming closer until he was standing in front of me.

"Derek, look, I'm sorry I–"

"Ssshhhh," he said, putting his forefinger finger to my lips. Then he kissed me. "Don't worry, I love you," he told me.

Teary-eyed, I feared for my life in that moment.

"I missed you, baby. Let's just spend some time together. Now, lay down on your stomach," he said innocently.

"Why?" I asked.

His face switched to an angry expression. "Shut the fuck up and do what I say!" he barked.

So, I did.

"Now just relax and don't think about nothing," he said, his tone returning to a soothing one.

I lost more control of my fear as he pulled down my pants and tore my clothes. Praying to be rescued, I started yelling, but my screams were soon silenced by his hand, which he placed over my mouth. My yells turned to whimpers.

"If you yell again, I'll kill you…and not in the conventional way," he spat, then pressed the gun to the side of my head. "I'll kill you like this."

It was the most horrifying feeling.

"If I pull the trigger, this bullet is going to go through your brain.

So, keep calm."

I gave in. My body started shaking. I was scared to death that he would pull the trigger. I was Nina, and I was tough. But, this was different. I was Nina, and I was raped before. But, this was different. I was legitimately afraid for my life! I was afraid of not coming home to my kids, of never seeing their beautiful faces again. I tried my best to stay and let him do whatever, because at that point, all I thought about was surviving so I could get back home to my kids. Before, I looked at situations like this as fucked up but sort of normal. This, however, wasn't normal at all. I kept disappearing deeper into my thoughts as he kept blurting things out like, "You like it, don't you, bitch? You like that shit" and "This was always your fantasy, wasn't it, you whore? Tell me you like this shit. I want to hear you say it." I played along, moaning as if I were enjoying it, but inside, I was just trying to stay in my head so I wouldn't scream or cry. After he was done, he got off me.

"You liked that shit, didn't you?" he barked again.

I just smiled back while trying not to break down in front of him.

"Why don't you get some rest, baby," I told him in the calmest voice I could muster. My plan was to escape while he napped.

"No, I'm going to take a shower," Derek said, then walked out the room.

That's when I broke down. See, I was right. Hell did return, and it was sooner instead of later.

After breaking down for a bit, I got dressed and ran out of the building in my ripped clothes. I could hear him running after me in the hallway. When I got outside, I hid out of sight as he came out and started looking for me. Seeing a cab parked a little distance from me, I ran up and banged on the window, looking distraught. I heard Derek calling out to me, so I jumped in the cab. The old man in the driver's seat turned around to look at me. Sensing that something terrible had just happened, he looked worried and shocked at my appearance. I'll never forget that man's face because he probably saved my life that day.

"Please, sir! I only have ten dollars on me, but can you please take me home? Like right now! I'm trying to get away from someone," I begged.

He asked me where I lived and took me home. He didn't even take my money. When I got out, he asked me if I was okay. I told him that I would be alright and thanked him for driving me. He told me that I should report whatever happened. I nodded kindly and smiled back, then walked into my home. My kids flung themselves at me as soon as I entered the door. Holding them in my arms, I broke down in tears because I had never been more grateful to come to them than I was at that moment. I was never more grateful to be alive than I was at that moment...and I don't think I had ever loved my babies, or anyone, more than I did at that very moment.

Chapter 18

After I put my kids to sleep that night, Tania and I sat on the couch sipping some wine, and I told her everything that happened.

"You have to tell the police," she said after getting over the shock of hearing my story.

"Oh, girl, I don't know," I replied.

"What! Why not?" she asked.

"Honestly, I'm just scared, girl. I mean, he's really well connected; he knows people. I was lucky to get away from him today. I don't want to risk crossing paths with him again," I responded.

"Yeah, I feel you," she said in a melancholy tone that expressed empathy for my situation. "So what are you going to do about the baby?" Tania asked after a small moment of silence.

"What do you mean, what am I going do? I'm going to get an abortion! I'm not going to have that psycho's kid now!"

"Okay, well, whenever you go, I'm going with you," she told me, her loyalty unwavering.

"Thanks, baby girl!" I said. "I'll call the place tomorrow and make an appointment. Right now, I'm going to head off and get some rest."

"Yeah, of course, after everything that happened. Get some sleep, baby girl," she replied.

I finished my wine and headed to bed. I didn't know how I would sleep after narrowly escaping death that day, but I was grateful to be home.

*****

The next day, Tania and I dropped off my kids to school and then planned to go to the clinic after that. After dropping them off, I was walking back to get in the car, when I saw another car up ahead. I stopped dead in my tracks. It was a very familiar car. How could I have been so stupid to forget that my perpetrator worked next door to my kid's school! Derek was sitting in his car, looking at me through the open window.

"Come here!" he called out.

I calmly ignored him and continued walking back to Tania's car, where she was waiting for me inside.

"Come here now!" I heard him yell, and when I looked in his direction, I saw him reaching inside his coat.

Terrified that he would pull out his gun on us, I went over to him.

"What?" I blurted out as I walked up to his window, trying my best to sound as nonchalant as possible.

"I know what you're trying to do," Derek said with a smile.

"What are you talking about?" I asked.

With the swiftness of a cheetah, he grabbed on to my dress and started yelling, "I know what you're trying to do, you fucking bitch! And it's not gonna happen! You ain't getting no fucking abortion!"

He kept tearing at my dress as I screamed and tried to get away. Tania zipped out of her car and ran over, trying to help me. She kept screaming at him to get off. He let me go and drove off. Guess he got scared that she would call the cops. Tania took me back to the car as I fought back tears. I was hysterical, so we decided to go home instead of going to the appointment. Tania picked up my kids that afternoon so I wouldn't risk seeing him again.

After putting my kids to sleep that night, I sat down with Tania again.

"So what are you going do?" she asked me.

"I made another appointment with a different clinic. Hopefully, he won't know this time," I told her.

"How do you think he found out about the one for today?" she asked.

"I have no clue," I replied. "Maybe one of the people that works there got news of my appointment and told him. How the hell should I know."

"Girl, you need to do something about this! You can't just keep looking behind your back everywhere you go!" Tania said.

"I know, but right now, I'm just concentrating on getting this abortion done. Once I do, hopefully, he'll leave me alone after that."

"Have you thought about what he'll try to do if he finds out you got one?" she asked in a nervous tone.

"It doesn't matter, girl. I'm not having this baby under any circumstance!" I voiced defiantly.

"Yeah, for sure. I understand," she said.

"Thanks a lot for picking my kids up today, sweetie. Do you mind dropping them off and picking them up until I get this thing over with?" I asked, almost begging.

"Of course, girl! Are you crazy? I'm always here for you, no matter what."

We hugged each other, and I nearly broke down crying in her arms.

"Thank you so much for everything you've done for me. You're the most amazing friend anyone could ever ask for. I'll never be able to repay you," I said, trying to fight back tears.

I could feel her getting teary-eyed, too.

"Stop it! We've known each other since we were little nuggets running around and tripping over shit. That makes us family. You don't ever have to repay me, but just don't fuck me," she said sarcastically, and we both started laughing through our tears.

"Don't worry, baby girl. I'm never going to mess up on you," I expressed as we cried together.

After that, I stayed home until the day of my appointment because I didn't know if he would follow me if I went outside. I kept distracting myself, hoping to get over the trauma of that day when he raped me at gunpoint. I kept trying to go over things in my mind of how our relationship started off so great and then twisted into something crazier than in a movie. I mean, how do people work that way? How can they be one person with you at first and then become another person later on? Are some people really that mentally unstable? Or are they aware of themselves and make it a point to play their way into people's lives so they can get something out of them? I know actors did that, but for people to actually be an "actor" off screen like that without giving a shit about the effects it will have on other people, now that's some scary shit! A two-faced psycho is the scariest of all.

Anyway, Derek ended up finding his way to me while I was at home, too. He called me. I didn't know it was him at first. Surprisingly, he called to apologize for everything that happened and tried to make excuses for his behavior, and so on and so forth. He even implied that he wanted to get back together with me. I tried to refrain from laughing and simply said, "I'm getting an abortion," before hanging up. He kept calling again after that, apologizing and trying to make amends. I hung up on him every call.

Eventually, he called and Tania picked up. She ended up speaking for me, telling him that I was getting the abortion no matter what and that I wanted nothing to do with him ever again. To her surprise, he said, "Fine, fine, whatever," and that he would leave me alone from now on to do whatever I wanted but wasn't going to give me any money to get the procedure done. That was fine with me. I didn't need his money.

The day came, and I finally got the abortion done. Thankfully, my health insurance covered the cost.

After the procedure, I was in a bad state for a while – physically, emotionally, mentally. I'd heard that having an abortion takes a toll on you, but it isn't like people tell you it's going to be. The experience was much worse! I didn't feel like myself anymore. I felt like another person. I felt empty, cold. The doctors said it was a common feeling of depression and would pass, but I had depression before. This was way different. I literally felt like an empty shell of who I once was, as if something had hollowed my insides. My personality, my thoughts, my heart, my soul. It's like everything that was Nina had been taken out. I fought through tears every day, hoping I would be back soon...or hoping I would die soon. Either one of those scenarios would be better than what I was experiencing then.

Tania continued to look after my kids for me, but I couldn't expect her to keep doing it. To my complete shock, my mother reached out to me. She told me that she wanted to check on me and that she missed me, but I wasn't too sure I believed her. I ended up telling her everything that happened to me and slightly broke down over the phone. My mother was silent for a little while and then sighed. A kind of sigh that had a sadness and an empathy to it for what I was going through, but also a hint of regret for what she was about to say. She offered me to come back home, at least until this passed. She said it would be easier than putting all the burden on Tania, and if I were at home with my kids, she would look after us. Now I believed her.

Chapter 19

I moved back in with my mother until I recovered from my abortion, which was a long, slow process. After the first few disastrous weeks of living like a ghost, I started to slowly feel better. I was relieved my post-op depression was ending; now I could finally have time to rest legitimately. It was weird being back home after having been away for such a long time, but honestly, I was so focused on recovering my mind and body that I hardly had time to pay attention. Then, a month before my 18th birthday, my mother decided to get me my own apartment. She told me since I was better, it only made sense for me to have my own place with my kids. I wasn't surprised that she decided to subtlety kick me out, but I was damn sure surprised she got me my own place. Although how she did it, I don't know if I'll ever find out.

So, I moved out (with my kids of course) and got a job to support myself. But, my income was barely enough for me to get by. All I was able to afford was rent, food, and my phone bill. My kids still drained the life out of me, but better them than my mother, although she actually kept in touch with me now. Tania still helped me out with the kids every once in a while, and my life slowly returned to having a sense of normalcy for the first time in almost a year.

I met a man in my building named José. He was Puerto-Rican, in his early 20s, about 5'6" tall, and had Latin features. He always said hello when he saw me. I just usually smiled back. He was a gentleman – always nice, respectful, held the door open for me, asked me about my day, etc. I could tell he liked me, but I wasn't ready to get into something after what I'd been through. I wanted to settle into my new life on Jerome Avenue. I can't say I didn't enjoy his genuine behavior, though; it was nice.

My new job was stressful, but I made good money working as a waitress. I loved it because it was flexible enough to let me pick my kids up. That was pretty much my whole life: work and kids. I rather have it that way than any crazier shit happening.

Tania and I hung out once in a while but mostly talked on the phone. I saw José around often, still nice and genuine. After months of playing cat and mouse with him, he caught me in the elevator one day and asked me out to dinner. I agreed to go out with him just for the hell of it. I wasn't planning on getting into a serious relationship but figured there was no harm in just dating. He seemed like a sweet guy, so I gave it a shot.

We went out to dinner, and I learned that I had more in common with him than Derek since he was from my culture. Unlike a lot of guys I encountered, he was very much a gentleman. He tried a little too hard to make an impression, though. I told him to relax, but he admitted to being nervous because he really liked me. I can't say it didn't warm my heart a little. His nervousness kept through the entire date, and I ended up doing most of the talking, which was a little of a flip-flop from my usual dates. Out of nervousness, he didn't kiss me goodnight either, but I thought it was cute that he didn't. His average Joe quality was something new and totally attractive.

We kept going out after that. When I told him I wanted to take this one really slow after the last one, he totally understood. We didn't get intimate until after a few months of dating, which was good for me. It was a good change of pace to wait for a while, because it made it much more intimate the first time we got close. I was more surprised that he was fine with waiting. Usually, most of the men I'd been with wanted to rush into the physical part. So, I was glad José wasn't pushy about that.

After some time, I introduced him to my kids, and they took a shine to him, too. It was easy to be together since we lived in the same building. After dating for a while, though, he said he wanted to move in with me. That was a little confusing since we lived in the same building, but his reason was because he wanted to always be close to me. I definitely wasn't ready for something like that yet, and again, he understood. So, we shoved that conversation aside and continued dating.

My kids started having questions about their dad. When he got arrested, I lied and told them that he went away and was coming home soon. I mean, what else could I do? But, now, it seemed like I was having to brush them off a lot. Therefore, I encouraged José to spend more time with them so they felt like they had a fatherly presence in their lives. Hopefully, it would lessen their thoughts and questions about Pito.

I began looking for better work, as I wanted to start saving up instead of living paycheck to paycheck. With the way my life had been going, I definitely needed a safety net – if not for me, then at least for my babies. Jason and Jessica started developing a little sibling rivalry, always complaining on each other about stuff and trying to win my affection over the other. It was messed up but totally cute, too.

All in all, I started feeling more normal than I ever had before. I guess having my own place helped. It was tougher financially, but in some ways, I felt freer than I'd ever been. That feeling of complete and earned independence made me feel good about where I was going and made me finally feel more confident about where I was in life. So confident that I started warming up to the idea of getting into a serious relationship. After a little while, with a confident smile on my face, I told José he could pack his bags and move in. He gave me a genuine smile back.

He moved in, and you know what? It wasn't as scary as I thought it might be. He was his usual, warm, normal self, and my kids dialed down the questions since they always had José to hang out with them. What a nice load off my back! However, having another person living with us made things tougher financially, so I asked José to get a second job, which he did. Except now, he wasn't around that much anymore. I was happy he was making money, but I started to feel like I was living alone again with my kids since I didn't see too much of him.

Soon, my mother started to impose more on my life. She figured since she got the apartment for me that she could come around whenever she wanted. Sometimes, I would come home, and she would be there with a few of her friends. It became really annoying after a while. I still barely saw my boyfriend because he was always working, and it had been a year already that we lived together.

One day, I found myself throwing up in the morning...well, more like three mornings in a row. Uh-oh! I knew what that meant! I sprinted to the pharmacy to get a pregnancy test, took it, and sure enough, I was pregnant.

Things were going okay with José, well enough to consider marriage at some point. However, having another kid would put more financial strain on us. I didn't want to go through another abortion, though. No way in hell! So, I told José and said I wanted to keep the baby. He agreed that we weren't fully stable for a third kid but also agreed I shouldn't go through another dreadful experience of having an abortion.

José started working even more so we could be more financially set. Unfortunately, I had to work less and less the further I went into the pregnancy, and after the second trimester, I stopped working entirely. My mother helped me out by watching the kids since she was at our apartment often anyway. I didn't know how we would handle it, but all I knew was that we were having a baby. Then, one day, I went for my examination done, and the doctor told me that I tested positive for chlamydia. Chlamydia. Chlamydia, huh? Wait, wait, chlamydia? Oh my God, CHLAMYDIA! No, that's not possible. How could I have chlamydia? José didn't have anything when we started sleeping together; I knew because he showed me the test results. I got tested after being with Derek, and I didn't have anything either. I hadn't cheated on José with anyone nor had I slept with anyone in between him and Derek. It didn't make sense. How could I have– Then it hit me like a shining meteor to my head, and I broke down in tears.

I wiped away my tears, and upset, I left the hospital with my two children, Jessie and Jason. I called a taxi and headed to José's mother's house where he was visiting. I told my two babies not to be afraid and that Mommy had to handle some personal business with José. As they stood beside me at the phone booth, I called José, and he came down from his mother's house with an attitude, confused as to why I was there. When I asked him why he cheated on me, he answered me with a very nasty attitude.

"Why the hell are you asking me that, you bitch? Just go fuck yourself! I don't care what you're thinking! I answered what–"

"Are you serious? You go out, cheat, and give me chlamydia, and now you're telling me to fuck off? You must be freakin' nuts to talk to me that way!"

José owned two vehicles, which were parked in front of his mother's resident. So, livid at his response, I climbed on his cars and started breaking his windows. José went after me and slapped me. I immediately attacked back. When Jason and Jessie started crying, I ran to my children, grabbed them up, and went home in a taxi. That day was horrible. José sent the police to my home, but I lied about what happened. Lucky for me, my story was convincing enough that the police believed me and asked José to remove his belonging from my home. Welp, there went my third relationship.

Chapter 20

I lay on my couch one day when I was off and the kids weren't at home. I was reflecting on how my life had gone up to that point. I couldn't believe I already had three failed relationships under my belt that resulted in a marriage, two kids, an abortion, being raped at gunpoint, and getting my own apartment. All of this occurring before I was old enough to drink. It's as if I lived backwards, experiencing all the adult shit first when I was young and then trying to get some of that innocent childhood fun back. I mean, how in the hell did I get here, and more importantly, why? Whatever it was, I was going to start working on getting my life on track. I thought it was going smoothly with José, but now, I was back to living the single life...except this time, I had chlamydia tagging along until I finished my medication!

José and I had one more conversation since that night when I confronted him. He apologized a hundred times and genuinely seemed sorry for what he did, but I couldn't fully forgive him. It's a shame because up until the discovery of his unfaithfulness, I viewed him as probably the best guy I'd ever dated. But, I suppose no one's perfect; we all have flaws. What José had in honesty, integrity, and warmth, he lacked in self-restraint. So, a bitch at his job was able to seduce him. Deep down, he was a decent guy, and I wished him the best. But, right then, my main focus was deciding what to do with this pregnancy. I vowed to never go through having another abortion, but honestly, I felt it was my only option at that point. I couldn't have another baby as a single woman. No way. I was barely staying afloat with the two kids I already had. Not only that, but since I had chlamydia, the doctor told me there was a good chance the baby might be born with some defect, and I knew I wouldn't be able to handle that either. So, while laying on my couch, I started crying endlessly, shaking and breathing heavily as I slowly accepted the fact that no matter what, there would be another abortion for me.

    A week later, I got it done, and right afterwards, I was regretful. Tania went with me and then brought me home. I cried all day while trying to distract myself to get over it. I find it sickening that there are people who think women actually enjoy having abortions. Yes, maybe there are some crazy-ass women who get off on getting abortions, but the majority of us do it as a last resort. It's really one of the most difficult decisions to make and the worst feeling in the world. Imagine feeling like nothing. Imagine feeling disconnected from yourself, from your body, from your mind, and from your soul. Imagine walking around like a ghost and randomly crying throughout the day, fighting the fact that there had been a baby–your baby–growing inside you. Imagine grabbing your stomach but then realizing there's no baby. Are you imagining all that? Well, it's a hundred times worse than you could imagine! Whatever you're imagining the experience would be, the real thing is more amplified and more depressing. It's so not fun! But, as time went on, I learned to cope. The first abortion was more horrifying than the second, and the third was still enormously painful. But, I recovered a little faster this time. I took it easy for a few weeks and didn't work much during this time. My kids kept me occupied, and like always, Tania was there to help.

Chapter 21

The days went by fast, and the nights went slow. My kids were getting older. As time went on, I slowly returned to my old life before Jose. A life that consisted of dropping my kids off at school, going to a housekeeping gig, picking my kids up, helping them with their homework, making dinner, tucking them in, and then enjoying a quiet night with a glass of wine before hitting my bed. Compared to my life before, this was a lavish celebrity lifestyle for me. Hey, when you only have a few things to work with, you try and make the best of them.

I saved a little money here and there when I got some extra gigs. I mostly used those savings to celebrate the holidays with my kids. Now that they were old enough to analyze traditions, I felt it was important for them to take part in them. My favorite holiday was Christmas, so that was a given. Every Christmas before, we usually celebrated at my mother's house since I was always there, but that was more of a family gathering than an intimate celebration between just us. My mother would call a bunch of relatives over, and we would treat the night like one big party, with my kids and me regulated more to the sideline of things. Of course, people asked me how I was doing with my kids and all that, but my mother made the night mostly about her, her food, and whatever new stuff she got her "flavor of the month" boyfriend to pay for. She would make it a point to get a new financially well-off suitor almost every month just so she could have things to show off at special celebrations. So, yeah, I was finally able to spend the holidays with my kids this time, and it was all about us.

At Christmas, I used my savings to buy them gifts and a small tree complete with a few decorations and lights. After spending the morning tearing through their presents, I took them down to Rockefeller, where they got to see the big Christmas tree on display. Then I took them around the city so they could take in all the festivities and decorations, even though we couldn't afford to spend any money. Once we went back home, I made them a nice Christmas dinner and dessert. Afterwards, we lit the tree, and I would sit in front of it while hugging my babies. We sat there admiring it and taking in its soothing warmth. It was a symbol of peace on Earth, and that was soothing to them, especially after seeing so much violence and chaos while growing up.

    Before they went to bed, I helped them put cookies on a plate and pour a glass of milk, then watched as Jessica carried Santa's snack to the table with Jason helping her to hold it. I couldn't help but smile while watching them from the doorway of the kitchen. I taught them all about Christmas and Santa. I figured after growing up to witness such a depressing reality, it would be nice for them to be comforted by a pretty, sugar-coated, make-believe story. For most kids, it's the opposite. They grow up living in a bubble and thinking all this crap is real, until they get slapped with real-life trauma as the world opens up to show them all its nasty little surprises. My kids aren't those kids. With them, it was pretty much the reverse. They lived in an adult life their entire childhood. Therefore, I felt it was best for them to retreat into a world of sunshine and rainbows, so as to forget the horror of the depraved "real life" they grew up seeing. Hopefully, they would be able to bury that shit deep down until later in life when they got strong enough to face it again. As their mother, I at least owed them that – the prospect of a safe haven, however temporary it may be. All kids need that, no matter what age they get it. It keeps them balanced. I wasn't that lucky, though. I never had a safe haven. I was born into a hard, cold life, and that shit kept up with me all the way until now. I wanted my kids to have something I didn't – a temporary little bubble of happiness.

The holidays were really the only time we actually had fun. All the other days, it was mostly school and home. They were good students, too. Better than I was at that age. And I was starting to get closer to them. I think it's because it was just us. I mean, it had always been just us, but they also grew up with my mother, my grandmother, and my uncle, who basically became a grandfather to my children. So, they weren't with me all the time to bond. Now it was pretty much us three against the world, and because of that, we became closer than ever. Still, I wanted them to make friends so they could learn to be more social. They were extremely shy and only let loose around me. I don't blame them, though. They probably inherited their trust issues from their parents or "learned" trust issues by watching us, whichever you prefer to think. I wasn't going to push them, but I hoped in time they would start trusting enough to have friends. Guess they needed to warm up to the world a bit first. I just wished the cold world would warm up back. Some people say it does after a while; others say the world just pretends to like you. Oh, what the heck! It is what it is.

Chapter 22

One day, I was walking home from the bank and went around to the back entrance. There parked on the corner was a big moving truck, and a couple of guys were carrying furniture in. I guess a new tenant was moving into the building. I squished through the guys and the big sofa they were bringing in and went up to my apartment. While walking up the stairs, I remembered that I didn't get my mail. So, I turned around and went down to the mail area. On my way back, I passed by the back entrance again, and this time, there was a third man helping the two moving guys. He was dressed in street clothes, though, and had a cap on. He looked like he was African American and in his early 20's. He noticed me walking and took a break to call out to me.

"Hey," he said.

I gave him a smile and turned back. He came up to me, stopping me in my tracks.

"Hi, I'm Rick. I just wanted to introduce myself. I'm new to the building," he said.

"So that's your stuff they're bringing in?" I asked.

"Yep. Today is moving day for me!" he replied with a chuckle.

"Okay, well nice to meet you, Rick. Good luck with the moving," I responded coldly, then continued walking.

"Wait. I didn't get your name," he said.

"Oh, it's Nina," I told him, turning around again.

"That's a really pretty name for a really pretty woman. Nice to meet you Nina." He smiled as I walked away.

I wasn't really in the mood to introduce myself, but my politeness sometimes got the better of me. Once inside my apartment, I started going through my mail. Later on, I left to pick up my kids. On the way out, I passed by the back entrance and saw Rick again. He was by himself this time.

"Hey," he called out to me again, smiling.

"Oh, hey. You still here?" I asked.

"Yep, I've been moving all day and just finished," he said. "The guys are bringing in the last thing."

"Oh okay. Went well?" I asked.

"Yeah, went smooth as butter," Rick replied.

"Good. Well, I have to go. So, see you around."

"Thanks. I hope I see you around, too," he said, then asked, "Wait, what apartment are you in?"

"Um, I'm on the third floor," I answered.

"Right, you don't want to tell me the apartment number." He smiled. "That's real smart. You have a good head on your shoulders."

"Yeah, well, growing up on these streets, you have to be smart if you want to get ahead," I replied.

"True story, true story," he said. "Well, I'm on the second floor. My apartment is 2B."

"Oh, so you're telling me your apartment. You don't think that's dangerous?" I chuckled.

"Well, for me, it's a little different. I mean, you're a girl, so you got to watch out for yourself. As for me, I don't think I'm in any danger by telling you where I live. I can handle myself." He laughed.

"Really! What if I'm some kind of psycho? Females can be pretty dangerous, too, you know," I shot back in a slightly snarky tone.

He laughed harder. "Oh, no doubt. You girls can be more dangerous than us guys most of the time. But, you don't strike me as that type of woman. You seem like a nice one to me," he said with a warm smile.

"The nice ones are usually the sneaky ones," I quipped back.

"Touché, honey," he said with a chuckle.

The Scars That Save Us

"Anyway, I have to go. So, I'll see you."

"No problem. Hope to see you around," he called out as I walked away.

I sighed as I walked down the street. I could tell Rick liked me, but I didn't know what I wanted to do about him. He didn't seem like the usual type from my culture. He seemed nice but definitely gave off a hint of a player vibe, as well. However, unlike a lot of players I knew, he seemed genuinely nice rather than just "player" nice, or in other words, being nice just so he could get what he wanted. I honestly didn't know if I wanted to get back into the dating world again. I felt it would've been easier if he didn't live so close, but with him in the same building as me, it would be awkward if I had to keep seeing him and constantly trying to avoid him.

*****

Later that night, I tucked my children in bed and went to relax on my couch. I thought about calling Tania to talk to her about Rick, but I pretty much knew what she'd tell me. He was handsome and seemed nice. She would definitely tell me to hop on the train. So, instead of calling her, I opted to go to sleep early since I had a gig the next day.

The next morning, I bumped into Rick while on my way out to take the kids to school.

"Hey, Nina. Good morning," he said with glee.

"Good morning," I replied.

Looking down at my kids, he asked, "Are these yours?"

"Yep," I told him.

"Wow! Did you have them when you were fourteen or something?" he said sarcastically.

"Yep," I answered while chuckling.

Oh, how he was unaware of the irony that I actually did have them around that age.

"Hey, little man. How are you?" he said to Jason as he held his hand out to him in an attempt to get a high-five.

Jason merely looked up at him with a bland expression.

"Sorry, he's a bit shy around strangers," I said.

Rick smiled and replied, "Oh, that's cool. No worries."

"Well, I have to get these two to school, so…"

"Oh, okay. Nice seeing you," he said.

"Yeah," I responded and went out the door.

*****

Later that night after tucking in my kids, I got on the phone with Tania, a glass of wine in my hand.

"C'mon, girl, you have to get out there already," she yapped after I turned down her offer to get together on Saturday.

"Look, right now, I'm just focused on my kids and work," I yapped back.

"Yeah, but your kids are doing fine, and you don't have a gig every day. I mean, I hardly see you anymore," Tania said.

Her comment made me feel like I had been neglecting my best friend.

"Well, look, I don't know. Maybe I have to get someone to watch the kids," I responded.

"My little cousin can babysit them," Tania quickly offered. "It's no big deal. And maybe you can finally meet a guy over there."

She chuckled, but I was far from amused.

"Listen, babe, I'm not trying to get back in the dating pool right now. I want some space, and I don't have time for no more bullshit," I quipped.

"Look, sweetie, you need to get back into the swing of things, Tania pressed. "You can still have your space. You don't have to get into anything serious, but going on a date every now and then won't hurt you. It'll only spice your life up a bit."

I gave a sigh over the phone, letting her know my annoyance. Then

The Scars That Save Us

I heard a knock on the door.

"Hold up, girl. Somebody's at the door," I said, then laid the phone down and went to the door.

It was Rick. I was shocked.

"Hey, sorry to bother you this late," he started.

"How did you find out my apartment?" I asked, surprised and freaked out somewhat.

"Oh! I saw you earlier when you came home with the kids. I took the stairs, and right as I passed by your floor, I caught you going into your place. I wasn't sure if it was you because it was for a split second, but I thought I'd give it a shot." He laughed.

"Don't you live below me on the second floor?" I questioned, my tone suspicious.

"Oh yeah, but I was with my boy, who lives on the fifth floor. So, when I came down from there, I caught sight of you right at the last second," he explained with a cheeky smile.

"Oh," I said. "Well, what's up? What do you want?"

"Well, I don't know how to say it, so I'll just be real. I would like to take you out to dinner?"

Now part of me wanted to slam the door in his face. Like how are you going to creepily show up to somebody's door at a late hour and ask them out instead of just doing it the next time you catch them in the elevator or something? I felt uncomfortable, but my politeness got the better of me once again.

"Look, you seem like a nice guy, but I'm honestly not trying to get into anything right now," I replied.

"Hmm, bad experiences, eh?" he said with a slight grin.

"What does it matter?" I snapped.

"Look, I'm just asking for one dinner, please. We go out and eat, and if you aren't feeling it, then we call it a night."

He smiled once more, and I started to get annoyed a bit. Mostly because I could sense his "player" attitude come out a bit in his persistence. In my younger age, I would've been drawn to that.

Nina Garcia

"Hey, you're Puerto-Rican, right?" he asked.

"Yeah," I responded and couldn't help but smile. "Alright, fine, one dinner," I said, finally giving in. *And here I go again.*

Chapter 23

The following week, we went out for a nice dinner while Tania stayed with the kids. This date was a bit different than what I was used to, in the sense that Rick was leading the entire night, trying to make a good impression with lines, jokes, and compliments. I guess because he was a bit of a player, leading a date with a woman came naturally to him. José before him was far more relaxed and more nervous, and Derek was more high-end sophisticated and stuck up, coming from an upper-class world. That's not to say I didn't consider Rick a suitable choice. On the contrary, Rick was confident, charming, and relatable as we were from the same culture. So, we had plenty to talk about and connect with. He was so confident in his craftsmanship that when he took me home at the end of the night, he thought he would go in with me to "see my place", but I set him straight. We continued to go out, and time after time, he kept trying, until about the fifth date when he charmed me enough to get me to go into *his* place. What can I say, I felt comfortable enough, and it had been a while since I was intimate with someone. When we went into his apartment, we made ourselves comfortable with foreplay, and then I asked him to get a condom.

"Oh damn, I don't have condoms."

"What do you mean?" I asked.

"I don't keep condoms because I haven't been with anyone in a while. I've recently been tested for every sexually transmitted disease, and my results were all negative. So, you don't need to worry," he answered.

"Why don't I need to worry?" I questioned with a raised brow.

"Because I'm sterile, and I'm good to go," Rick replied.

"Huh?" I responded.

"I became sterile because I was into body building," he explained.

"Oh...really," I said.

"Yep. Why do you look creeped out?" He laughed.

"I'm not. I'm just surprised. I never met a guy who was sterile before and so careful with himself," I told him.

"Yeah, it was one of those dumb mistakes I made while bodybuilding with consuming steroids, but I made sure I was good to go otherwise," he said, then leaned in closer to me. "Believe me, Nina, I'm not ready for a kid right now."

Afterwards, we kept seeing each other, and he seemed like a genuine, cool guy. He told me that I was the first woman who he wanted to take seriously. I didn't know whether to buy it or not. But, I figured I would keep him at a distance so if things didn't work out between us, I wouldn't be heartbroken like the times before.

Life at home continued to be routine and more or less relaxed. My kids were doing great in school, which made me extremely proud. The best thing I wanted for my kids was to get a good education. I didn't have that chance because I made a lot of dumb mistakes, such as getting pregnant at the age of fourteen and getting married before I finished my schooling. But, with the life I was raised into, who could really blame me? I mean, my home life was so depressing and miserable that the only way I could think to escape it was to bypass the teenage years and go straight to being an adult with a partner and family. Little did I understand back then that there was no way to bypass the teenage stage, that it would still continue, except now I had a partner and a kid to add to my responsibilities on top of doing the "growing up" thing. This indeed made it harder instead of easier. Wanting my kids to have the chance I didn't get, I tried my best to be a good mother and make their home life as loving as possible so they wouldn't have the excuse of wanting to fuck up their lives in order to escape their hell.

The Scars That Save Us

Life was also a bit better now for me personally since I had Rick to enjoy it with. From time to time, he took me out, and he was nice to my kids, playing with them whenever he came over. I wasn't sure if I wanted to make it a serious thing yet, as I liked having the emotionally-distant but physically-fun relationship. However, things were going good. I'd rather have our relationship be good than push it into complicated territory.

One day, I was working a gig at a private house. No one was home. I had been cleaning all morning and was down to scrubbing the floors. Once I finished, I would pack it up and go pick up my kids, but I started feeling a little lightheaded. I figured it was probably from all the cleaning. So, I took a break, drank some water, and then continued scrubbing. The lightheadedness didn't go away, though, and then I started feeling dizzy. I went into the bathroom to regain myself. Something was wrong; I felt sick. Something was going on inside me; I sensed it. And then it came. I started vomiting all over the bathroom floor that I had just cleaned. Figuring I was probably coming down with something, I decided to ignore it and finished cleaning as fast as I could so I could get the hell out of there. After I picked up my kids, I went straight home but felt woozy throughout the entire journey. Later that night, I felt a little better, so I dismissed what happened to me as simply having an off day. But, something inside me was wrong. I felt it.

The next day, I dropped my kids off at school and decided to go home since I didn't have a gig booked that day. On my way, I started feeling it again – that sick and woozy feeling. I decided to make an appointment with my doctor when I got home. However, on my way home, I suddenly threw up again! All over the curb this time! I couldn't dismiss it anymore. I couldn't make excuses. My experience wouldn't allow me. My experience with wooziness a few times before kept trying to drill harsh reality into my brain while my denial kept fighting back, but I couldn't fight it no longer. I had to give in to the wisdom I gained from my experiences and accept what was happening

Nina Garcia

to me.

    I instantly ran to the nearest pharmacy, crying all the way there, unable to comprehend the shock of what it was but refusing to acknowledge the fact that it was possible. It was impossible. How could it be possible? I ran in, grabbed a pregnancy test, and ran home. As usual, I went into the bathroom and started the process of crying while hoping I just caught some sort of bug that had symptoms eerily similar to morning sickness. As I sat on the toilet seat, I waited for the color on the stick to show up...and it did.

Chapter 24

"Why did you lie to me?" I shouted while pounding on the door until Rick opened it.

"Whoa, whoa! What the hell are you talking about, Nina?"

"You told me you were sterile!" I shouted.

"I am," he replied, looking confused.

"Really! So how the hell am I pregnant?!"

His eyes widened. "What?!"

"Yes! I started feeling sick, so I went to get a pregnancy test, and that shit is positive! I'm pregnant!" I snapped.

His eyes widened even more as he stood there frozen.

"You're...pregnant?" he asked, seemingly in denial.

"Yeah, and here's the proof!" I said, shoving the stick into his hands.

He looked down at it in shock.

"And you're the only man I've been with in the past few months, so the only explanation is that you lied to me!"

He kept looking at the stick in shock and then finally looked up at me.

"But, Nina, I didn't lie to you. I *am* sterile," he said.

"So what you're saying is that I'm lying? That this is someone else's stick, or that I got pregnant by someone else? Well, I didn't, and you know I'm not like that!" I snapped.

"No, of course I know you aren't like that. I'm not saying any of that. I'm just saying I'm as shocked as you. I mean, this can't be possible. I became sterile five years ago, and I haven't gotten any woman pregnant so far. So, this just isn't possible. It has to be some mistake," he said, confused.

"Yeah, well, it clearly isn't a mistake. I took the test twice. This stick is the second one, and the first one was positive, too."

He kept looking at me in shock.

"So, either you aren't sterile anymore, or shit, you've just been lying to me."

"Nina, I swear to God I'm not lying! I'm sterile!" he said in defiance.

"Well, I don't know what to tell you. I guess you're not anymore because I'm pregnant. So, congratulations! It looks like you're going to have your first kid!" I snapped at him, then walked away in anger.

*****

I was queasy throughout the whole day, so much that I almost threw up while cooking dinner. For the third time, I was pregnant. Yet, I found myself more unprepared for it than I'd ever been. Not only was this unplanned, but it felt a little...twisted. I mean, the guy I was sleeping with was supposed to be incapable of impregnating me, and yet, it had happened. I wasn't sure if I could trust that he was telling me the truth. I couldn't bear the thought of having another abortion, so I didn't even let myself consider it an option. And if Rick was truly lying to me, then this baby would be born out of a devastating loss of trust, which would destroy our chances of being a couple.

After tucking my children into bed, I went to relax on the couch. I tried to push the whole thing out of my head, but there wasn't anything to distract me. Nothing except my TV and my phone! Well, you guessed it. I picked up the phone faster than I had in ages and started dialing Tania's number. Just as I did, I heard a knock on the door. (Dun, dun) I put the phone down, forgetting I had just dialed Tania, who answered on the other line. I was nervous as shit. I had a feeling I knew who it was. Yep, I saw Rick though my peephole. I really wasn't in the mood to talk to him, but who knows? Maybe he was coming to give me an answer that would help ease my anxiety about how this all happened. Maybe he would confess some shit. I didn't know the reason for his visit, but I would soon find out.

"Hey," I said after opening the door.

At first, he just stood there looking at me like a zombie. After a few pauses, he asked if he could come in, and I let him.

"What's going on?" I asked.

He turned around after a bit, and I didn't recognize him. He looked totally different. He had an almost hateful, vicious aura about him, but it wasn't in full effect. It was like he was transitioning between confusion and anger.

"Are you okay?" I asked.

"That baby is not mine."

"Excuse me," I said.

"That baby is not fucking mine!" he spat, then continued walking into my apartment.

I followed him because I sensed something very terrible inside him and wanted to be able to get to the phone in case I had to call the police. The whole time he was walking in, I'm pretty sure I heard him keep muttering, "That baby isn't mine." Once we got to the living room, he turned to face me.

"Rick, c'mon, stop. You're scaring me. What's going on? Let's talk," I said in the most inviting tone I could muster, but his look didn't change.

"Did you fucking hear me, bitch? That baby isn't mine!" he barked.

"Excuse me? Don't call me that, alright? Now sit down and let's talk," I said, trying to stay calm.

"No! That baby is not mine! I'm fucking sterile! I know it! There's no fucking way this kid is mine!"

Shocked by his outburst, I started to back away.

"You fucked somebody else, didn't you? You fucked somebody

else behind my back, and now you're trying to pin this kid on me," he barked again, looking at me with vicious eyes.

"Rick, baby, stop. I swear to you I didn't. Let's just sit and talk, alright? Relax," I said, faking calmness as best I could.

"No! That baby is not fucking mine!" he bellowed, then smacked me across the face while calling me a bitch.

I fell to the floor. Then, with both hands, he lifted me up and slammed me against the wall, sliding me up to his eye level.

"You fucking bitch! You opened your pussy to some other nigga and got fuckin' pregnant! Now you gonna pin that fucking kid on me so that you can milk me for child support! Is that it, bitch? Huh?" he barked like a mad dog.

While in his chokehold, I gasped and tried to tell him that what he thought wasn't true.

"You think you so smart, huh, bitch? You must have been goin' through the day thinkin' you a fucking genius, right?"

As I clawed at his hands that were around my neck, he slammed me onto the living room floor. I scrambled to crawl away and regain my breath.

"Listen, Rick...baby, please...I didn't fuck anybody else. You know I didn't," I panted.

"Yeah, right! I thought I knew you! I thought you were different than those other bitches I used to fuck with, but it turns out you're just like them!"

I continued to crawl away, putting some distance between him and me.

"I know your kind too well! All those bitches from the hood do the same shit! Using their uterus like a fucking gambling chip! Fucking dumbass, broke-ass honeys don't know how to do nothing but get knocked up by different guys and milk money from each one while turning them on each other! Those hoodrat bitches got their own little business! And they make mad money from it!" he barked.

"Then maybe you should stop fucking with those bitches!" I

The Scars That Save Us

barked back. "I ain't no dumb bitch from the hood! Got it? I'm a grown woman who has been through enough pregnancies not to pull all this dumb shit on you! Got it? If I wanted to do that, I would've done it with some other nigga before, not with you! I'm not a hood bitch, so you need to stop treating me like one!" I snapped, remembering my Latin roots.

That's when he came up to me and stomped me back to the ground. As he delivered punch after punch, I heard my kids screaming and managed to get a blurred glimpse of them from the corner of my eye. They had run out of their rooms in a haze of worry and into the living room. They screamed for him to stop. Ignoring their cries, he shoved his boot onto my face. Jessica kept screaming at him to stop, but he just kept digging that boot in. He dug so hard I thought he would crush my face under the weight of it. To tell you the truth, I was more scared for my kids. I mean, if he killed me, who knows what he'd do to them. He wasn't violent towards children, but would he want to leave witnesses to his assault. He wasn't himself at the moment, and I started wondering if maybe he was on something. Regardless, I shuddered at the thought of what might happen if I lost consciousness or even worse died.

Then I felt the weight of his boot lifted off me. He picked me up and went with me to the wall. He pushed me against the window so hard that the few bottom pieces of the glass broke off. He quickly picked up one of the pieces, and I'm sure my horror showed on my face.

"Don't worry, bitch! I'm not going kill you!! I'm not a fucking murderer! Especially since you're all your kids got!"

I could feel myself about to black out. My children's screaming became more and more distant. I closed my eyes, not believing it all led to this. Everything I'd been through had led to this shitty moment, and apparently, all because I got pregnant by mistake through no fault of my own. I can't believe this was actually going to happen to me. After all the hell I'd been through and overcame in my life, this is how my life was going to end? I could not believe this shit. What did I do so wrong? I hadn't been a saint, but was I really so bad to deserve this?

And then, I woke up. I was on the floor, bruised and bleeding. My vision was blurry, but I was able to see a few police officers carrying Rick out of the apartment in handcuffs, dragging him across the floor as he was yelling and fighting back. Then my kids blocked my vision. They both came to me and helped me slowly get up. They cried as they hugged me.

"Mommy! Mommy, you're okay! Thank God!" they said while sobbing in my arms.

Extending my arms to hold them slightly back from me, I asked them what happened.

"Mommy, I was so scared you were going to die," Jessica began. "Then the police came in and pulled him away before he tried to kill you. They were fighting with him and trying to arrest him, and you dropped to the floor! Oh, Mommy, we were so scared! We thought you died!"

"Calm down, baby. Relax," I told her as she continued to cry. "Who called the cops?"

"The neighbors," answered Jason.

I smiled while cradling my two children in my arms and hugging them tighter than I ever had. I never felt more grateful to be holding them, so I wanted to cherish the moment. I never felt more grateful to be alive, so I wanted to savor the moment by wrapping my arms around the only two things that ever gave my life meaning. I sat there cradling them, smiling, and sobbing with them.

Chapter 25

I spent the next day in the hospital recovering from my wounds, while Tania stayed with my kids. The doctor told me that my injuries wouldn't affect the pregnancy, and I was relieved to hear him say that. I still had other wounds to recover from, though, and I'm not talking about those from Rick's kicks and punches, but the emotional wounds.

After I returned home, I went and got an order of protection against Rick but was still scared since we lived in the same building. Yeah, he was arrested, but I suppose someone bailed him out. So, he returned to the same vicinity where I was living.

When my mother found out what happened (probably from Tania), she gave me a call, sounding more comforting than she had in a while. She offered for me to move back in with her so I would feel safer. In any other situation, I would've turned her down, but since my psycho ex lived pretty much next door, I accepted her offer. I decided to stay in my apartment until I had my baby since it was already near the due date, and then I would make the move. Because it was close to the time for me to deliver, I didn't take any more gigs either. I stayed at home mostly, recovering, and asked Tania to pick up my kids from school. With more free time, I started packing so I could be ready to move my stuff in my mother's when the time came; I also used my time to do some deep reflecting.

I reflected on recent events, trying to slowly pass through the trauma of my experiences. When I started dating Rick, I thought it would be easier since both of us were from the same background. I had no idea Rick had a monster side to him. Now I was even more terrified of having this baby. What if my child inherited Rick's dangerous side? I know the whole "nature vs. nurture" argument has been endlessly debated, but now it was very real and absolutely terrifying for me! How could I base my pregnancy on a total gamble? Sure, I could raise the child right and all that, but what if it didn't work? What if the child had too much of Rick in them? All these questions plagued me, but still, I couldn't bear the thought of having another abortion. I wanted my baby.

Besides reflecting on the pregnancy, I gave an ample amount of thought to my relationships and all the nasty lessons they taught me. I tried to think about why I made certain choices and whether they were really rooted in how I was raised, or should I say lack of being raised. Did my empty relationship with my mother contribute a lot to my poor choices? Oh, I was sure of it! But did I have another path to travel? What if all my future choices were made based on how fucked up I ended up being from my upbringing? Is this how it would always be, constantly making bad decisions because I didn't know any other way? Would I pass that nature on to my children, making them just as fucked up as I am? Nothing I reflected on provided me with answers, just questions and anxiety, wondering if I would ever get through it. All this reflecting and paranoia made time zip by, and before I realized it, the day came when my water broke.

*****

Five hours after arriving at the hospital via ambulance, I gave birth to a perfectly healthy baby boy. Unfortunately, Rick was present the whole time of the delivery, which I wasn't too happy about. But, of course, kind-hearted Nina couldn't say no.

My kids came with Tania to see me at the hospital. They were ecstatic about seeing, holding, and playing with their baby brother. Tania was all smiles as they swapped him from one set of tiny arms to another, fighting to hold him. I felt a lot better now that I had him, but

I had to stay in the hospital for a bit so they could do some tests.

Tania and I talked about what I would do now with three kids. I told her I would move back in with my mother for the time being. She offered for me to stay with her, but I told her I didn't want to impose and that my relationship with my mother was a lot better, which was a lie. Once again, she asked me how I would handle three kids.

"Tania, honey," I replied, "out of all the shit I've been through in my life, my kids are the least of my burdens. I'm sure I'm strong enough to manage one more in the collection," I told her with a smile.

Smiling back, she replied, "I know you are. I just wanted to make sure that you knew it."

I slowly smiled back.

Chapter 26

Oh God, what a head case! This little thing! It had been a week since giving birth, and I was still reeling from the whirlwind of it all. I was at home the whole week, taking it easy. It was wintertime now. My kids were at school, and I was enjoying the alone time with my baby boy, who I named Justin. Yes, he was adorable but still a head case!

A week after my discharge from the hospital, I moved in with my mother. I still wasn't fully recovered from delivering my son, but I had to leave since I had given my landlord notice of me moving out. To my surprise, my mother was a little happy to see me. Not overly happy like a parent usually would be to see their child, mind you. It was more like a subtle kind of happy, as if she missed me somewhat. Or maybe she was just tired of being alone. I couldn't tell, but she helped me settle in with my kids. She was much happier to see her grandchildren, and they were happy to see her.

Life hadn't changed much at my mother's home; it was sort of nice being back home. Not because the people were nice, but because it felt familiar and safe. My mother had moved from my childhood neighborhood, so life at my mother's house was fairly simple only because I was so accustomed to the bullshit. Every day I would spend time with Justin while my kids were at school or sometimes with their grandma.

After a little recovery period, I decided to pick up a job as a real estate assistant so I could start saving up some money. It wasn't consistent work, but it was fine for the time being. I enjoyed learning from a good real estate broker friend of mine, who taught me a lot about the real estate business and was very helpful with arranging everything for my new apartment.

My mother stayed with Justin whenever I had to work. She was a little different than I remembered her. More relaxed, more peaceful towards me and the kids. Maybe the loneliness got to her while I was gone. Truth be told, she never really had somebody love her as much as me, despite the fact that I hadn't loved her that much at all. And my brother? Well, he never really cared for my mother. So, the little amount of love or affection she experienced from me was pretty much all she ever had. I wasn't sure what to feel more, sadness or pity. I suppose both. But, maybe after I left, she finally realized what she had lost. Or maybe she found a new respect for me after I showed her that I was able to live on my own. Who the hell knows? I knew one thing, though. I wasn't going to be there forever. So, for now, regardless of whatever was making her more warm towards me, I would take it.

Chapter 27

Justin was getting bigger by the day. At two months old, he was quite the happy little boy, always laughing and smiling. So far, it seemed he didn't inherit any of his father's personality, and that put my mind at ease.

I was working more regularly now and building up a good amount of savings. Things at home were pretty peaceful the entire time. My mother helped me a lot and mostly stayed out of the way when I didn't need her. As for my brother? Well, you know... I was pretty content with having this period of peace. It's something I sorely needed.

After I lost a little of my baby weight, I started getting hit on more by both men and women! But, I had no plans of going down that road again. I'd had enough of relationships. I'm not the type to say never, but at that time, all I wanted to focus on were my kids and the foreseeable future for my life. (I know I've said that before but...whatever! Keep reading!)

I talked with Tania a lot, considering the fact that I couldn't go out with her because of my new baby. She was annoying sometimes when the conversation of men came up, though. When I told her my stance, she tried to get me to change my mind, telling me that I didn't need a relationship but there was nothing wrong with having a little fun and fooling around with men. But, I'm not really that type. I was always the monogamous relationship kind of gal, committing myself to one person at a time. Since Tania didn't have the same upbringing that I did, she couldn't understand. But, when you grow up having bad experiences with sex at a young age, and having grown men defiling you for their own instant gratification...yeah, it kind of turns you off the whole casual sex thing. At least for me, it did. I wasn't going to spill all my demons in hopes that she would leave me be, though. Instead, I just brushed off the topic and redirected the conversation to more important things, such as where was I going to go next. Not just regarding my current living situation, but life in general.

I didn't just talk about this with Tania but also with myself. Every day, all throughout the day, I would try and figure out where I was going to go with my life from this point. Of course, the next logical step would be to find a place for me and my kids, but then what? Continue working an unfulfilling job as a housekeeper until they go off to college and then be left to live alone? Is that all my life would amount to? Would working as a housekeeper even be enough to support me and my children, considering that everything increases in price due to the economy. Before I got by because I usually had a partner, and our combined incomes would take a huge load off of me when it came to the household expenses. But with me having sworn off relationships, that wasn't an option. So, as you can see, there was a lot to figure out.

I decided I needed some advice, and ironically, the only other person I knew who had once been in the same situation as me was my mother. A single parent, she wasn't a career-minded woman, but she made it work while raising my brother and me. So, I thought I'd go to the expert. One night, after putting my babies to bed, I saw her sitting on the couch with a glass of wine in hand.

"Hey, Mom," I started, sitting down next to her.

"Yeah?" She turned to me, waiting for me to continue.

"I need some advice on a few things, and I thought, if you're not too busy, I could talk to you."

She looked at me with an awkward expression on her face, almost as if she was shocked by my request.

"You want to get advice...from me?"

"Well, yeah," I answered. "I mean, is that okay?"

She paused for a few seconds, looking baffled that I would ask her for advice on something. Hell, I was just as baffled for asking. Truth be told, this was probably the first time I ever did.

"Go ahead, girl. Shoot," she said with a half-smile.

"Well, I've been thinking about my life now with three kids and how I'm gonna navigate things from here, and well, you were pretty much in the same place. Even though you had two kids, you raised us on your own without a stable career. So, I was just curious as to how you did it. You know, how did you manage it all?" I asked as neutrally as I could.

There was a long pause before she finally answered.

"Well, I have to be honest here. I'm pretty surprised you're asking me about my parenting since you always claimed I did a bad job of it," she said with a hint of attitude.

"Yeah, and I still stand by that opinion," I expressed, annoyed at her response. "I'm not saying you did a good job raising us, but you still did the job nonetheless. I don't even know if I'm gonna do it better with my kids, but I just figured maybe you had some method of doing it, and… You know what, forget I asked. Sorry to bother you."

As I stood to leave, my mother grabbed my hand to stop me.

"No, wait. Look, I didn't mean to snap. I just… I was just caught off guard, that's all," she said.

I was pretty surprised at her for not defending her parenting. Did she somehow come to terms with the fact that I was right? Nah, that couldn't be it.

"Okay, well, do you have something you can tell me then?" I asked as I sat back down.

"I don't know. Maybe. I mean, there wasn't really a formula to anything. I just made it work. I took jobs wherever I could. I spent my money right and managed expenses. I mean, there wasn't some golden plan. I just did what I had to do," she answered.

"So that's it? You just found your way by winging it?" I asked.

"I wouldn't go that far to say I winged it," she said while laughing.

"Don't forget that I also had many men helping me, sometimes for a little while and sometimes for longer term," she added.

There it was. The catch. I almost forgot that my mother used to be a serial dater and that almost every man she dated had big wallets.

"So is that why you kept dating rich guys, so they could support you financially?" I asked with a grunt.

"I wouldn't say they were all rich. Maybe a few of them were, but they were all well-off enough to help me with some finances while I dated them," she answered.

"Yeah, but you never really had anything serious with any of them! So was money the whole reason you kept doing it?" I asked with a hint of anger.

"Now hold on! Just because I never had any serious ones doesn't mean I didn't try. There were a few who I got close to and had affection for. I really liked a few of them, but it's not always easy to maintain. I won't lie, though. A lot of them I kept dating because they were helpful. I was only thinking about how to provide for you guys, and I ended up doing it way more than I initially planned because it was so easy. You know what I used to look like in my prime. I had dogs throwing themselves at me left and right," she finished.

"Yeah, I remember, but let's go back to the part where you were doing it for us. I clearly remember you coming home with shiny jewelry and brand-new clothes every week, and you were always replacing furniture," I snapped.

"Hey! Yes, I tended to myself, but I thought of you and your brother, too. Don't pretend I didn't! You were both always taken care of, weren't you?" my mother said.

"I mean, yeah, I guess. But still, you don't think what you did was wrong? Using men, leading them on, letting them get attached, and then helping yourself to their bank accounts! You didn't feel you were a bad person for taking advantage of people?" I snapped with a morally serious tone.

"Wait, wait! Hold on! Who told you I was leading them on?" she asked.

I paused. "Well, weren't you?" I asked, confused.

My mother paused and looked at me while slightly shaking her head. "No, baby, I did not lead them on...because you're right, leading someone on is wrong. Every man that I had a relationship with – be it short term or not – always knew what cards were on the table," she told me.

"Really?" I asked, genuinely surprised.

"Yes, I always made it clear to them where we stood. I didn't play them. I don't think it's fair to string someone along," she said.

I have to be honest. I was quite surprised to hear my mother preaching some level of moral groundwork.

"So they were fine with dating you and helping you out financially even though they knew they weren't heading toward anything serious with you? Why would any guy do that?" I asked with a suspicious tone.

"Well, it's not as simple as that, Nina. It's a little more complicated."

"How so?" I asked.

"Just because I didn't lead them on doesn't mean I kept reminding them about our expiration date. You need to understand that sometimes things are better left unsaid. I'm not saying I planned an ending to each relationship, but I didn't plan for the future with them either. I let things take their natural course. I didn't bring up exclusiveness, and I didn't mention a short-term timeframe. I didn't say much of anything really. I just focused on being in the moment with them – having fun, joking around, going out. After we got to know each other well, I would bring them over to stay the night, make them breakfast in the morning, this and that. When I needed a little help paying a bill or buying something, I asked them, and they almost never said no. Then when our relationship started to run its course, I ended it amicably," she explained.

"So you just kept everything on the down low," I said.

"In a manner of speaking, yes. I didn't lead them on with any false promises, but I didn't set rules around the relationship either. I just played things as they went. Sometimes I did it because I really liked the guy, and sometimes because the guy was fun and willing to help me out financially," she finished with a slight smile.

I sighed. "Still, you don't have regrets about going around like that?"

"What for! I didn't commit no crime. I just got carried away with that lifestyle, that's all. I ended up getting comfortable in it too much past my stay, but I did what I had to do to get by. I took care of the house and my kids. There was no crime in what I was doing, Nina, and many others do the same thing," she argued.

I sighed once more. "Alright. Well, thanks for the talk," I said, while getting up to leave.

"Sure. Hope it helped," she replied back nonchalantly.

Yep, I definitely had to find my own way to making it. I was not prepared to go into the life that my mother lived. I had too much self-respect for that. Even though I'd been through a lot of bullshit, way more than I deserved, I wasn't the type to swing through men and exploit them. That wasn't me...or so I hoped.

Chapter 28

After recovering for a while at my mother's house, I returned to work. The housekeeping thing was more steady now. With my kids back in school, I concentrated on working as much as I could so I could save up and move out soon. Don't get me wrong. Life was good living at my mother's house. Far better than I expected. But, if I were serious about standing on my own two feet and not following my mother's way of life, I had to have my own place. I refused to mooch off her, even though my mother would ask me to help her with the finances. Plus, it would just be healthier for my kids overall to be in our own home. I didn't want to chance my mother's toxic influence rubbing off on them. I wasn't sure where I would go from there once I got my own place again, but that's why it's called taking baby steps. I was going to take the first step and figure out the rest along the way.

One day, I came home from work and fell asleep on the couch. God, I was tired! As soon as I closed my eyes, I drifted into a deep sleep and started dreaming. My dream transported me through a timeline of past events like I was on a magic carpet ride – remembering my childhood, being married to Pito, having my babies, overcoming toxic relationships and psychotic encounters. It was like experiencing Nina's greatest hits mix of good memories and terrible ones and was probably why I usually didn't sleep well; I seldom got a restful sleep after everything I'd been through. I'll say this, though. If my "greatest hits" session that I was experiencing that day was a legit album, that shit would've sold millions. Then I was woken up by the sound of the doorbell. I sleepily scuffled out of my bed, made my way to the door, and opened it. I must have still been dreaming because there was NO WAY the person standing on the other side of the door could've been there in real life. My mouth fell open, and my eyes almost popped out of their sockets.

It was Pito! I couldn't believe it. My first love was right there in front of me. He looked shocked, as well, but in a good way.

"Mi amor," he said with an angelic tone.

"Pito?" I gasped.

How could this be? I gave myself a few slaps in the face to try and wake me up, but he was still standing there smiling at me.

"Nina, my love, you're still here! In the same house! After all these years!" Pito said as he scooped me into a hug.

I was so shocked to see him that I couldn't even hug him back. I pushed him off, closed my eyes, and slapped myself on both cheeks again.

"What are you doing?" he asked.

When I opened my eyes, he was still there. That's when I knew it wasn't a dream.

"Pito! Are you really here?" I asked, aghast.

"Yes, I'm really here, mi amor," he replied with a chuckle. "What, you think you're dreaming? It's really me, don't worry."

Forming a half-smile, I asked, "But how?"

"Well, they let me out early for good behavior," he explained. "I wasn't sure if you were still living here, but I thought it was worth a shot, and I chose right!"

"Wait, so you're out? That's it?" I asked, shocked.

"Yep! I'm out for good, baby! I'm back, and I wanna be back with you!"

With that statement, I fell from the cloud I was on and crashed to the ground like a meteorite.

"No!" I snapped.

His face dissolved from euphoria to shock almost instantly. "Wait, what?"

The Scars That Save Us

"No way, Pito. Sorry," I said, shaking my head at him.

"Why?" he asked, seemingly unbelieving of my answer.

"Why?" I snapped. "Why?! Maybe it has to do with the fact that I had to watch you be dragged in handcuffs, with our kids beside me, after finding out you robbed a fucking store! Remember that?" I shouted as he started to look ashamed. "Maybe it has to do with the fact that for most of our marriage you sold drugs on some corner while I stayed at home taking care of the family and waiting for your ass to come home, hoping it would be in one piece! Or maybe it has to do with the fact that I always worried that you would get arrested or put me and the kids in danger!" I continued, while he tried to get in a word. "Maybe it has to do with the fact that we barely had sex, even when you were home! Maybe it has to do with the fact that you were never there to help out with the kids. And don't tell me it's because you were out providing and shit, because you didn't do a good job of it! Maybe it has to do with the fact that we never spent time together, or maybe it was the fact that you went to another woman!"

I finally stopped, out of breath.

"Okay, okay, you're right!" he barked. "Yes, I was that person, and I'm sorry, amor. I am so sorry I hurt you in all those ways. "I'm not defending none of it. I own up to everything, but I'm a different person now! Don't forget that I did years in prison, and that really changes a person. During all that time, I had the opportunity to think, reflect, and gain perspective on things. I did programs and read the bible among other shit," he shared.

"Oh, really! You read the bible?" I asked sarcastically.

"Yes! I read it every day, and that stuff gives you much insight into a lot of things. The point is I'm not the same person anymore, Nina. It's a whole new me, and I wanna show you him."

I looked at him suspiciously.

"Okay, look, forget about getting back together. That was stupid of me to mention in the first moment of seeing you after ten freakin' years!" he said, laughing at himself.

"Yeah, I'll say. You were never the bright one when we were together. I guess that part didn't change," I commented, and we both gave a small laugh.

"I bet a lot has changed around here, though," he said.

"Yep, it sure has," I replied with a sigh.

"Okay, well, is there a place we can go to at least talk? You know, catch up and stuff?"

I thought about it for a moment. "Yeah, I guess," I finally said.

I figured what harm could it do for us to catch up. I mean, I hadn't seen him all those years, and I had missed him. So, I called my mother and asked her to pick up my kids.

"C'mon, let's go," I said, grabbing my keys and leading the way out the door.

*****

We sat in a café in our old neighborhood. Pito and I used to go there frequently when we were younger, but the look of the place had changed after the new renovations. It still had a nostalgic feel to it, though.

"I can't believe we're back here." Pito smiled.

"I know. Brings back a lot of memories, doesn't it?" I said, smiling back.

"Yeah, it does, but it's way different now," he responded, then sighed. "Bigger," he added with a laugh.

"Yeah, well, it's been ten years. A lot of stores have changed their appearance. You're right, though. It's definitely bigger." I laughed.

"Remember the picture that used to be on that wall by the cashier?" Pito asked.

I looked in that direction and smiled. "Yeah, the two pizza boys making cheese with the lady chef, and they all had goofy-ass smiles," I said, and we both laughed.

"And their mustaches curved too far up," Pito said as he continued laughing.

After we calmed down from laughing, we sat there in silence for a few moments looking at each other, seemingly in a better mood after reminiscing.

"So you have a third kid now, huh?" he said rhetorically as his face transformed into a serious state.

"Yeah, his name is Justin," I told him.

"And his dad's not around, right?" he asked.

"Nope. His order of protection is permanent, but just to be safe, I still gave up that apartment and moved back here," I said.

"Good. Better to be safe than sorry," he said. "That's one thing I'm proud of not doing, never getting violent with you," he said with a half-smile.

"Yep, you never touched me. That's definitely one of the things you did right."

"But you know I never would anyway, right?" he continued. "I mean, I ain't that kind of person at all." He gave me an empathetic stare as if trying to signal to my inner trauma.

"I know you're not, Pito. That motherfucker Rick was a straight-up monster," I told him.

"He deserves to have his balls cut off for doing that shit," he expressed angrily.

I smiled at the snarky irony of his statement, remembering how Rick had tried to convince me that he couldn't have children.

"So how are Jason and Jessica? They okay?" he asked.

"Yeah, they're great now. I mean, they obviously shared in some of my traumatic experiences, but I tried to shield them as best I could so they wouldn't be affected by my shit too much, you know," I replied.

"Oh, definitely. I don't blame you. If that was me, I would straight up make them live in a freakin' bubble until they went off to college," he said with a chuckle.

"But, all in all, they're good. Far better since we've been living with my mom. Jessica is already turning twelve soon. Jason is hitting puberty, complaining to me that he's growing hair on his face and shit."

We both laughed.

"And he's spending more time in the bathroom now," I added, giving him a nod that was meant to be taken as a signal.

Aghast, he closed his eyes and awkwardly giggled. "Oh, God."

"Yep, it's getting to that time, Pito," I said, smiling.

"So they're doing good with your mom, you say? That's kind of surprising."

"I know, but she's always been better to them than she ever was to me," I said with a regretful tone.

"Yeah, I remember," he replied.

I sighed. Not wanting to open up that can of worms again, I changed the subject.

"So you got a lot of help in prison, eh?" I asked, bookmarking all he had told me about his time locked up.

"Absolutely! That shit changes you! Like I said, I did a hell of a lot of thinking and reading. I was seeing a therapist in there and all that! Why do you think they let me out for good behavior?" he said.

"Well, that's good. I'm glad it bettered you and affected you positively."

"For sure, for sure," he responded. "I just can't believe all the shit you've been through while I was locked up," he continued, sounding shocked. "Thank God you managed to get yourself together after everything."

"It's definitely been a crazy ride, Pito." I sighed. "I'm just glad our children are safe after everything, and Justin, too. He's such a normal, adorable, and innocent child – the total opposite of his dad, which I'm extremely happy about," I said.

"Me, too. Our kids are everything to us. I thought about them and you every single day while I was locked up," he expressed with a longing.

The Scars That Save Us

"Really?" I asked, smiling.

"Absolutely, mi amor! All I ever wished was to see all of you again when I got out. And I understood why you never came to visit me. I knew how angry you were, and I didn't want the kids to see me in there either. I didn't want them to see their dad as a failure. So, thank you for that, Nina," he said in the most sincere tone.

"You ain't a failure, Pito," I told him. "You just fucked up. We all make bad choices. I wasn't exactly a prize for them either, you know."

"Well, I'm glad they had you all this time rather than me. I'll always rather they have you in their life than me. I mean, you're like the best woman I've ever known."

"Really?" I said, not fully believing it.

"Of course! Yes, I made the stupid mistake of cheating on you and stuff, but that never changed my opinion of you. I knew you were way better than the woman I was with. I was just with her because I was the one who was weak at that time. But you? You were always better than any woman I ever met. I just should've showed you that more," he expressed.

"Really?" I asked, fully believing him now.

"Yes, really," he said with a smile.

"Thanks. That's sweet," I said, half-smiling.

"I mean, you never cheated on me even though I cheated on you. That right there should tell you how much better you are than me."

He laughed, and I smiled back. Then he looked to my left again.

"Damn, I miss that painting! It was always my favorite one," he said.

His laugh descended to his smile, Pito's signature smile, the one I fell in love with. God, that warm smile still hadn't changed. Damn! He and I entered a cycle of nostalgic expressions, both towards each other and around the café, complete with pauses and occasional seconds of awkwardness here and there. It was all smiles nonetheless as we tried to stick to the good memories of our past.

"You know, I'm really glad we got to see each other again after all these years," he said, smiling.

I smiled back. "Me, too. I missed you."

"I missed you, too, mi amor."

I saw it in his eyes that he really did change a bit. Maybe not by much, but something definitely was different. He looked down at his watch, and I sighed.

"Alright, look, if we're gonna do this, it needs to be for real this time," I said sternly.

He looked up, baffled. "What?"

"I'm serious. If we're gonna give it another try like you want, then we need to be in it for real," I told him.

"Wow, really?" he asked, surprised but seemingly happy.

"Yes, really, but only if we're in it to make it work. No experimental bullshit! No test run like it was before. I'm serious, Pito! No more drug dealing, no more hustling, no more fucking around, nothing! If we gonna do this, it's gotta be for real."

"Yeah, of course! Absolutely!" he replied.

"It's just gotta be me, you, and the kids. That's it. We both get a good job, and we come home to each other. We focus on us, and that's all. If we do this again, it's gotta be for life!" I stressed, trying to drill my message into him clearly.

"I would love nothing more," he said with a big, warm smile.

I smiled back after hearing that. I wasn't sure if I was making the right move (and kind of doubted I was), but if he got released early and found me, then maybe there was some fateful reason to all this madness. So, I looked at him longingly because I had missed him. At the same time, I was suspicious because I wasn't sure about him. But, alas, I gave another sigh and started to get up.

"C'mon," I said.

"Where we going?" he asked.

I turned to face him and smiled. "I see prison definitely didn't change the fact that you're still an idiot."

He gave me a confused smile, half-giddy to hear my humor again.

"You're about to go see your children, you stupid herb. Where else?" I said.

His face lit up like he had seen a pair of tits. "For real?"

"Yeah, for real. Now, c'mon! And remember, it's been years, so they're asses are grown now, which means you better make a hell of an impression. And try not to act stupid, you fuckin' doof!" I said, smiling and walking away.

As he got up and followed me, I knew he had a wide smile on his face, the one that showed all his teeth.

*****

We came home, and I opened the door to lead the way into my big reveal. My kids were playing right near the hallway, Justin was asleep in the corner, and my mother was in the kitchen washing dishes. My kids looked up upon my arrival, all smiles as usual, but their expressions quickly turned to shock when they saw who popped up behind me. At first, they were confused, trying to recall who it was since they were both very young when they lost him. But, after they realized who the man was, they stood there shocked as if they had seen a ghost. My mother looked up, and when she realized it was Pito with me, she dropped the dish she had been washing. Aside from the sound of the dish breaking as it hit the floor, all was silent.

Instead of giving an introduction, I decided to simply smile. I figured it would tell them everything they needed to know. Pito gazed at his children as if he were watching them come out of my womb for the first time. Then he slowly smiled as he crouched down and opened his arms. Jessica and Jason, as if by instinct, started to run toward him and jumped into his arms at the same time with such force that they all nearly fell backward. They were smiley and almost teary-eyed. Upon seeing their reaction, I became emotional myself. I was rarely an emotional person, but I didn't anticipate how much this scene would really affect me. I mean, this was my children seeing their dad for the first time in years. Regardless of what I thought about him, seeing their overwhelming reaction to his arrival filled me with joy. I was happy for them, and instantly felt better about my decision.

My mother walked over to me. She was more shocked than happy, but I could tell she pretty much understood what happened...and what was going to happen. She stood by my side, watching them, and then leaned over to me.

"I hope you know what you're doing this time," she whispered.

I smiled and replied, "Yeah, I think I do."

Chapter 29

A month later, Pito and I were living our lives together. We got a new place, an apartment of our own. He got a job getting paid under the table to do deliveries for a furniture company, while I worked as a fulltime cleaning lady. Our kids were doing great. They seemed to feel better with Pito back in their life, and he took on the responsibility of taking care of Justin, as well.

We decided to flush everything that we went through while separated down the tubes and start fresh. We wanted to pick up where we left off before he got arrested that night all those years ago, and it was working…at least for now. I mean, we were different people now, but there was an air of familiarity, albeit a faint one. Still, it was nice. It was nice to be with someone I knew instead of having to learn a stranger. It felt good to be with someone who I knew wasn't going to hurt me, physically anyway – someone who shared in my past, knew me, and had been through some of my most vulnerable moments with me. Most importantly, it was nice to be with the father of my children so they didn't have to get accustomed to someone new again. Bottom line, it felt like I had my family back.

Pito and I were at the point in our lives where people actually DID get together and start families because they'd had enough time to grow and gather life experience. And even though we did it a bit backwards, at least we were doing it RIGHT this time by having our own place, our own space, and being the appropriate age! It's as if we were having a rebirth of sorts, a second chance at life and marriage. Maybe, just maybe, this was the new beginning I was always supposed to have as opposed to forcing the one before.

*****

Months went by in our smooth-sailing life, and after tucking my kids in one night, I thought about surprising Pito. He told me that he was going to stop by a pub after work and have a few drinks with one of his co-workers before coming home. So, wanting to spice things up, I decided to go out and buy some new lingerie to wear that night. I purchased something tasteful to accentuate my boobs and butt. On my way back home, I took a different road and went to the pub instead. I don't know why, but my intuition told me to check in on him. So, I went into the pub, and there sat his co-worker, Juan, with a beer in hand

"Hey, Juan," I said, walking up to him.

He almost choked upon seeing me.

"Hey, Nina! Wasn't expecting to see you," he said, shocked.

"Yeah, I didn't really expect to come, but I thought I'd surprise you guys. Where's Pito anyway?" I asked.

"Oh, he's in the back," Juan replied. "I think he got a little too drunk," he added with a chuckle.

I laughed at his comment and then proceeded toward the bathroom. The whole time I was walking, I hoped Juan wasn't right and that I wouldn't have to carry Pito's drunk ass home. As I stepped into the men's bathroom, I dodged greasy drunktards and ignored their disgusting comments about the size of my boobs and the motion of my butt.

"Pito, are you in here?" I called out from right inside the doorway.

I heard a sound in one of the stalls, and something in my gut told me to investigate. So, I moved in the direction of where the sound had come from and opened the door. There was Pito leaned up against the wall, his pants open, cock out, and a drunk bitch on her knees in front of him, deep-throating his shit! I couldn't believe it! There it fucking

The Scars That Save Us

was again. Just as I was getting comfortable in a newfound beginning for the umpteenth fuckin' time, that asshole Life popped up like a Jack-in-the-box and decided to scare the shit out of me with its usually twisted appearance. Seriously, Life, you need to get a new hobby, dude, because I did nothing so horrible to deserve you enjoy twisting me in circles so much.

Anyway, the bar hoe pulled off when she noticed me staring at them. Pito was half-asleep as he turned to me. When he slowly realized who I was through the veil of alcohol's spell, his eyes widened with terror, and he started zipping up his pants.

"What the fuck? What is this?" he asked, acting as if he were clueless to what was going on.

My blood started to boil at an almost uncontainable level, but somehow, I was able to hold myself mostly due to the confusion. The confusion and my Anger-Denial-Acceptance thought process were the only things stopping me from going full on Carrie.

"I could ask you the same shit?" I summoned the anger to blurt out. "Oh God, you pitiful fuck! Less than a month back together, and here you are getting your five-inch churro sucked by this greasy bathroom cunt! Please tell me you just got too drunk and didn't realize she was emptying your nuts!" I barked.

"Hey!" yelled the three-dollar whore.

Without a second thought, I smacked her right across the tiny stall, and she slammed onto the toilet seat.

"That's right! First, you cleaned my boyfriend's sac. Now clean the fucking toilet seat, bitch, while we talk! Puta de mierda!" I yelled, then turned back to Pito. "Please tell me you didn't realize it, Pito. Please tell me you were just too damn drunk!" I begged.

Leaning against the wall of the stall and with his head down, he gave a half-smile. Then he looked up.

"Okay, I knew the skank was all over me. She even came to me before I got to the bathroom and pushed me in, and I didn't do shit, alright," he slurred in a low tone.

Nina Garcia

Despite my eyes being filled with tears, I didn't sob due to the anger.

"Why?! Why would you do this to me, Pito?! You swore to me that you were a changed man and wanted to make this work for life! Did you just lie about all of that, Pito? Why would you do that? For what? Why did you do this? Fucking why?" I angrily sobbed, the clear vibe of the Anger-Denial-Acceptance cycle present in my voice.

He looked down; his partial smile had now grown into a full smile.

"You wanna know why?" Pito said, looking up after a short while. "I'll tell you why!" he continued in a slightly angry tone. "Because all those years in jail opened up my eyes, alright! They opened up my fucking eyes, bitch! They opened my eyes to how fucked up life is and how unfair things turn out! I busted my ass hustling and working to make bread for my family only to get fucking caught in the end, which resulted in me losing you, losing the kids, losing my life, and losing my money! That's what I got for everything I went through! Then I had to endure a ten-year sentence in prison that's pretty much a hellhole for people like us! Those motherfuckers that sat behind the desks hate browns, blacks, and anyone who doesn't look like them! Every day, the guards beat on me! I got pissed on! I had niggas do sexual shit to me! I ate shit! Every. Fucking. Day!" he shouted, spittle flying out of his mouth.

"I asked myself constantly what did I do so wrong to deserve all that!" he continued. "Why did I lose everything? And then...then I had a fucking epiphany, or whatever the fuck you call it! Like I told you, jail time changed me. See, I realized that life is random. That's it. That was the only explanation for why life turned out the way it did for me. Because it's just motherfuckin' random! And I came to the conclusion that in order to enjoy it, I had to live it up and just enjoy myself instead of playing by the rules. I had to live life to the fullest. So, to answer your question, no, I didn't lie to you about how I felt. I really did want you and the kids back. That was all true. But, what I also told myself when I got out that shit bowl is that I would not miss out on shit and

The Scars That Save Us

enjoy life to the fullest. So, I would make it my business to take care of y'all, but I would also take care of me by making sure if an opportunity came my way to have a bit of fun that I wouldn't turn away from it. That's what I did wrong before! I sweated myself and got fucked in the end! So now, I'm just gonna focus on working, enjoying my life with you, and enjoying my life outside of you! All that make sense, huh?" he finished.

I didn't know what to say. I was overcome with so many emotions during his drunken rant, and none of them were good. But, as I stood there looking at him, I no longer felt betrayal, or anger, or even shock. What I felt was simply pity. Pity for him most of all. Pity for what he used to be and what he had become – the love of my life and now a miserable bastard filled with delusions. Then came the moment that I knew what to say.

"The only person this makes any sort of sense to is you, Pito, and that makes me sad most of all," I voiced with regret.

"Then I guess we good here," he said, laughing.

Now my rage came back into the fold.

"Not yet," I replied with a smile of my own.

Then I lifted my arm and swung it like it was a bat and I was playing baseball, knocking him right in his face. He smashed into the wall of the stall. Again, I swung at him, this time with pitbull rage, and straight-up clocked him. I hit him so hard that blood flew across the air and splattered the walls. Screaming from the pain of the blow, he slid down to his ass, the blood still spraying out from the gash on his face. His blood sprayed all over the girl's tits, and some landed on her lips, where drops of his cum were still drying. As she started screaming, I punched her back onto the toilet seat, and then I started slapping both of them. I gave each a couple of hard slaps, while yelling out "Usta mierda despreciable! Eres una puta despilfarradora! The slut continued to scream throughout the whole thing.

I assume one of the bouncers heard the commotion, because he entered the bathroom looking as though he was ready to earn his paycheck. When I started walking out, he tried to stop me, but I kneed him in his groin and pushed his head onto the edge of the sink. His jaw smashed that shit and down he went, also bleeding onto the floor.

Pito pushed her aside and came crawling after me like a zombie, making sounds and shit. I walked out in a fit of rage. A few guys got in my face and tried to hit on me. Not in the mood, I fisted one in his nose, and the other, I took a nearby bottle and broke it across his face. The shards of glass pierced his left eye as he let out a brutal scream. I pushed my way through the crowd as they all rushed over to the two men to see what was going on. I stormed out and walked my Latina ass home. Fuck the bullshit!

Chapter 30

As tears forced themselves out from my angry eyes and flowed down my face, I busted into my house. Pieces of my broken heart were chipping off little by little, breaking from the inside. My rage barked at my heart like a tormented pitbull, scaring it to stop crying over what happened, telling it to stop being a pussy, and threatening that if it didn't stop bleeding over Pito, my heart would be cut out. My heart was so scared by that pit bull that it was forcing itself to tear so it could disappear from me. I don't think I've ever had such a conflict between my anger and my pain. Those two emotions were like two siblings fighting each other over me, trying to see who should overcome the other and take over, trying to test who should be the new favorite child of mine.

I had an urge to take every glass bottle in the house and throw them in every direction, but I remembered my babies were sleeping. Instead, I went to the bathroom to wash my face. While staring at my reflection in the mirror, I tried to accept another failed relationship, but this was different. This was Pito, not some random stranger. This was my first love, the father of my kids...and it failed yet again!

Oh, you pathetic, naïve bitch! How could you fall for that shit? Why would you believe it would work again?

What do you mean why? Because he really did seem different. He was back, and he was different.

Oh, shut the hell up, girl! Just because he seemed different didn't mean it was a good kind of different. Seriously, what the fuck is wrong with you?

Oh, shut the fuck up! I did it, okay? I held on to hope.

Well, there you fucking go, bitch! You "hoped". Don't you get that shit is a fucking illusion.

Oh, so what? I'm supposed to live without hope?

No, you're supposed to have hope, but also be fucking smart and realistic. THAT'S what you're supposed to fucking do! Not make a mistake and then cry to me in the mirror afterwards. Stop making fucking MISTAKES! How many times do you have to get hurt to learn that, bitch?

Yeah, well, it's too late now. It's done. (sobbing)

This is done, yeah. But the future is NOT done, alright? So, try and think about shit next time! You hear me, girl?

Yes, I fucking hear. You're right, and I'm sorry, okay?

No shit, I'm right! Aren't you the bright penny?

Alright, shut up already. I don't need this right now.

Girl, you won't ever need to hear it if you just think more next time, that's all.

After battling it out with myself in the mirror and letting out a good sob, I went and lay down on my couch to continue processing the recent events and the grief that came with it. I couldn't believe what happened that night actually happened. I mean, just a month ago I was reunited with my childhood love and ex-husband, which I didn't think would ever happen again. Now I was right back at square one faster than I'd ever been. How could it be? After everything I'd been through, you'd think I would be used to this by now, but this wasn't just another relationship with any ole guy. This was my Pito, who suddenly came back into my life after almost ten years. Before he showed up like some kind of godsend, I had sworn off ever having a relationship again. I believed the rest of my days would be lived out as a single mother and then an old bitch with cats. But, then he came back to me, and I looked at it as some kind of sign. Maybe he was the one I was truly supposed to be with, and the other guys were just failed experiments in order to send me that message. Maybe this time it was meant to work since we were older and wiser.

But, hey, I guess that's how life plays ya. It can't do it if you're pessimistic, so I guess it sends you good signs on purpose to hype you up and make you believe it has something good in store for you in the end. Then once you become hopeful and start trusting life again, it knocks you back down. I started to realize that's exactly what this was – life's game. Life wouldn't be able to have its fun if you didn't get pulled into its game. Well then, I was just going to have to stop falling for it. After promising myself over and over not to fall for life's tricks, this was what I needed to finally drill that promise into my head. Not the failure of another random relationship, which usually still left me with a sliver of hope for the next one to be better. The failure of another chance with Pito is what I needed to finally seal the deal of my hopelessness.

I started thinking about the conversation I had with my mother about relationships. But, this time, I replayed it using my mother's perspective. In an attempt to understand where she was coming from, I went back and forth between my replies in the conversation and her replies. That's something I was unable to do before, but I found it far more easier to do now. I started to interpret my mother's words differently and understand her advice differently. I now understood her advice to me was based on her experiences in the dating world. It started to make sense to me why she had the opinions she had about relationships and why she handled them the way she did. Not letting herself get attached and treating each relationship like it was a business partnership. You know, where each partner only stays in the business as long as it benefits them and they are getting regular returns from the other partner. But, as soon as they stop getting benefits and returns on their investments, they leave the business and break the partnership. It was genius and so very simple. I'm sure she tried the romantic and emotional approach for a few of them like she told me, and like me, she probably ended up getting an education from life's unsparing curriculum. And that's why she decided to try and be smarter than life by playing men for their wallets. She provided the physical benefits of a relationship as long as she received the monetary benefits. No broken hearts, no consequences, only gains.

I suddenly understood it all. I saw things though her eyes. I interpreted life through her perception. It was so much different than my view, and yet, that's what started to draw me to it – the fact that hers worked and mine didn't. Then it hit me that maybe I should take my mother's advice, even though I promised myself I never would. That promise belonged to the old me, though...the one who was the butt of life's jokes and object of its manipulation. I didn't care anymore about the rebellious need to go left everywhere my mother went right. I only cared about what would help me lift myself up from the scourge of the bully that pushed us all around – reality!

I only cared for fulfilling the needs of my children and myself. I wanted to live my life with no strings attached; I wanted to be free. I wanted to be happy...and I wanted nothing to do with men anymore beyond the gains they could provide in a superficial-based relationship. I'm not saying I wanted to set out to punish innocent men intentionally. I just didn't care for men anymore. I didn't care about connecting with them and forming relationships. No, I was going to take what I needed and move on with life, and hopefully, my future partners would be on the same page.

It was time to make a change and create a good reality for myself. I made a promise to myself to never let life or men push me around again. Instead of sobbing and telling reality to stop hitting me, I would fight back from now on.

Chapter 31

Okay, first things first! How do I do this? I didn't exactly have any experience being a playgirl or anything like that. All of the relationships I'd ever had happened because the men were the ones who were courting me, and most of the time, I wasn't even interested. It was only after heavy persistence and sweeping me off my feet that I gave any of them a shot. Now that I think about it, I never threw myself into a relationship, and I sure as hell never dated casually. So, now, I would have to flip everything. I would have to be the one to dive into the dating world, ignite interest, face possible rejection with confidence, and actually make it seem like I gave a shit about a romantic pursuit even though it was a total lie. It was a little scary to be honest. It's not like I had anyone to show me the ropes, and I wouldn't give my mother the satisfaction of thinking I was taking pointers from her life. So, asking her was out of the question. But alas, changing oneself requires work. Where to start?

I decided to give myself a test run by going to the usual spot for catching fish – a bar, of course. So, that night, after putting my kids in bed, I dressed up real nice and fancy, tits bulging out and everything, and put on some makeup. Then I walked to the nearest place I knew.

I sat comfortably at a half-empty bar counter, sipping a mojito. The place was a little more high end than the cheap pub I broke noses in the other night. It looked nicer, more spacious, and cleaner. The bartender was even more jovial and calm. But, mind you, there were still some dirtbags in a few corners, acting all alpha and catcalling the females. I wasn't sure how I was going to steer what would be my first attempt at a casual conversation with a male stranger, but I guess the only way to find out is by taking the first step. I thought it best to use this bar as an experiment for me and not have any expectations. *Yeah, that's it!* That plan made me feel much calmer. I would just feel things out, and if I didn't feel it, pack it up and go home. *Good idea, Nina!*

Anyway, I continued sipping my mojito calmly. I tried looking around the bar every now and then, figuring anyone who caught me looking around might see it as a sign that I was fishing and would come over. But, it was my first time, and I was still shy. So, I'm sure I didn't seem very approachable. But, that's the beauty of a test run, though. I didn't have to give a shit about how anything happened. Just ease into the environment, and if nothing happens, I could skedaddle. No expectations! No giving a shit! And then I heard, "Hey, how you doin'?"

The voice came from behind me. I turned around and saw a random guy taking a seat on the stool next to me. He was black and looked to be in his 30's. He was dressed in street clothes, but not so street as to make me flip him off and not so cheap as to make me roll my eyes. In truth, I wasn't sure what I was looking for in a man, but I at least wanted someone presentable.

"My name's Deshawn. I noticed you looking around, and you looked kinda bored. So, I thought you could use some company," he said, sounding sincere.

"Oh really? And you didn't think for a second that I may have been looking to see if someone I was meeting came in yet? Are you really so quick to take it as a sign for you to come and talk to me, and that I need to be fucked?" I snapped.

I couldn't help myself from being defensive.

"Sorry. Didn't mean to bother you," he said, visibly disgruntled.

I instantly shut my eyes out of embarrassment. *Good going, Nina! You're supposed to be inviting and welcoming conversation! The old you used to flip guys off like that! You gotta remember you can't do that anymore if you wanna start this change! Train yourself to new tricks!*

After realizing what I did, I opened my eyes and turned around to see him starting to walk away.

"Wait!"

He stopped and turned around.

"I'm sorry," I started. "I didn't mean to snap. I wasn't waiting for anyone. I'm just a little tired, that's all."

He looked surprised at my reaction.

"Go ahead. Please, sit down. My name is Nina," I finished, forcing a small smile.

He smiled back, oblivious to the tension in me.

"Nice to meet you, Nina," Deshawn said as he sat back down.

Deshawn was nice. We had a good conversation, and I agreed to go out with him the following week. He was flirty but not in a gross catcalling way, which was a nice. But, again, I was trying to get to a different place. I wasn't trying to build up to any relationship. I would see how my experiment with Deshawn went and determine things from there.

The date came and went. Deshawn was absolutely trying to woo me, but I just accepted his subtle signals with a mix of forced interest and casual indifference. I enjoyed his company, though, because as I said, he wasn't giving off a bad vibe whatsoever. Then again, they rarely do in the beginning.

We got physical after a few dates, which was uncommon for me, and I wasn't sure how to respond at first. I mean, I wanted to sleep with someone since I hadn't in a while, but at the same time, he was still someone I was getting to know. In short, I had to force myself to react in a way that he would feel I was reciprocating interest in him, and I ended up enjoying it a little more than I thought I would. It was still unlike me to jump into bed with someone that fast, but again, I had pledged to start changing my ways when it came to men. I would play the game before they played me! And it didn't hurt that Deshawn was a good lover, too.

We started seeing each other regularly - and sleeping together regularly - and the fact that he seemed like he felt much better now proved that getting me in bed was his main objective when he came up to me that night. I did not complain, though. It would've been awkward for me if he wanted to get serious, because then, I would've had to navigate the dizzying map of how much information/signals to let out. I didn't want to get serious with him, but I didn't want to lose the casual thing I had going, either. So, his indifference worked for me.

Then came the time, a few weeks later, when I would finally (and subtly) ask him to assist me with purchasing some new clothes for my kids. I remembered what my mother had told me about having her casual boyfriends assist her financially. So, I thought I'd give it a test run and see if I had the same chops to work it like that. I could've definitely used some help with my rent, but we had just started going out. So, there was no way I was going to ask him to help me with something like that so early on. Hell, he'd run the fuck away! Therefore, I had to start small, and I figured new clothes for my kids would be the perfect test.

It was a Saturday, and after I tucked my kids in early, we went out to a Greek restaurant. The food was great, the place was nice, and we were talking about our week (as if I gave a shit about any of it). I was a little tense about how I would do this. I mean, it was my first experience trying to pull off something like this, and I had no tips or clues to go by. I could end up giving him the wrong idea and lose him completely. So, it was nerve-racking and rather terrifying. I tried to keep my cool throughout our conversation, trying to suppress the tension in me and be consistent with the nonchalant tone that I trained myself to use when speaking with Deshawn. Then, after he mentioned the great fun he had with me the last time, regarding to a sexual escapade, I saw my opportunity.

"Hey, Deshawn," I started.

"Yeah," he replied.

"I wanted to ask you for a favor."

"Sure, babygirl. What's up?" he asked.

"Well, it's just…I gotta get my kids some new clothes 'cause they ended up tearing some of their old stuff and…well…I'm real tight with money now since I just paid my rent and all. So, I thought…since we're seeing each other, you wouldn't mind helping me out with that."

I tried mapping it out as casually as I could. I didn't want to give a mini speech for fear that he would suspect it was rehearsed. So, there it was! Either he would catch the bait or send it flying back in my face. As I waited for him to answer, he just stared at me while continuing to chew the souvlaki in his big-ass mouth. He then lifted a finger to let me know to hold on until he gulped down his food.

"Sure, no problem," he finally replied.

I let out a huge breath of air, but I did it extremely slow so as not to give away any tension. It worked! Phew, boy, I felt relieved…and grateful.

"Thanks a lot," I told him.

"Yeah, absolutely. I mean, if you were asking for a pair of gold earrings for yourself or some shit, I'd probably be like we gotta wait six months. But, since it's clothes for your children, that's fine," he commented with a chuckle.

"Thanks. Good to know," I said while slightly laughing.

"Like you said, we're seeing each other, and even though it ain't serious yet, we're still pretty much together. So, anytime you need help with money, don't be afraid to let me know. If I can afford to help, I have no problem doing so."

I smiled back as warmly as I could. "Thanks so much. You're awesome!"

I smiled to myself, feeling accomplished, more confident than I'd felt in a while, and excited at the possibilities that were now open to me with the new lifestyle I was starting.

Chapter 32

Hahaha! Oh my God, I love you! I told myself while staring at my reflection in the bathroom mirror and having my first conversation with the new me. *I'm loving this! I love you! You were so on point!*

Yes, I was, wasn't I?

Yes! Yes, you were! I can't believe it! I can't believe how awesome I feel now!

Well, I told you, didn't I? You kept fucking ignoring me, bitch, and now that you took my advice, you see I'm always right.

You are! You are! Deshawn and I have been seeing each other for months now, and he's been helping me even though we're not serious! I could drop him at any time and feel no obligation. It's the best feeling ever!

Yeah, and to think of all the time you wasted on dumbass relationships, being a wife and shit, getting stomped on left and right. I always looked at you in the mirror and told you to change, told you to let me out so you could have a better life, but you never listened. Now you're saying thank you, aren't you, bitch?

I am! I am! Thank you! Thank you! Thank you! I can't believe how stupid I was before for not letting you be free. I love who I am now! I love the new me and how confident you make me feel! I love how I don't have to be committed or tied down anymore and that I don't have to care about men anymore! I love it! You're the best thing that ever happened to me!

Yeah, well, let's just hope you'll always be smart now, bitch. Listen to me, and you'll be good.

Nina Garcia

I will! I will! I laughed. *I'll never ignore you again! From now on, it'll just be me and you! You are now free, and I'm never going to suppress you again! Never! I love you so much! I love my new life! I love it all!!*

I laughed with myself in the mirror a bit more out of pure joy. I was so happy that I started to sob. This was me; this was my new life. This was the best I'd ever felt, and I wasn't going back to the old me.

I was living it up in my new ways. I still had Deshawn, and we were still casual. But now, I had Carlos, too! We met a month ago and hit it off. Both he and Deshawn helped me with my bills, while giving me enough space that I felt like I had my own life. Even though I had two semi-boyfriends, I was freer than ever. *Why stop there?* I thought.

I met Miguel at a gas station, and he seemed to really have it in for me. He was hitting on me while I was filling up my car and offered to pay for my gas after I was done. That already let me know he would have no objection to paying for anything I wanted if he was that willing to take care of an expense before he even knew my last name. But, I declined his offer, thinking that if I appeared too easy it would be a turn off down the road. Instead of taking his money, I told him that he could take me to dinner, and he was ecstatic.

We went out. While he was excited and salivating for my pussy like a dog, I was distant and patient like a cat. After training him to also be patient, I opened up my legs eventually and ended up getting "another one" under my belt! Miguel was far more generous than the other two, though. He helped pay my rent, bills, and anything else I needed. And that was within the first three months of knowing me! The best part was I didn't feel bad with any of them. I mean, I didn't tell each one about the other one, but each of them knew that what they had with me was a casual deal. They didn't expect any obligation from me nor I from them. They simply enjoyed having me and showed it by aiding me with whatever I needed (cough *paying for shit* cough). And I gave them whatever they needed (cough *pussy* cough).

Time went on, and my relationships became more of a juggling act. Some stayed, some got tired and left, and new ones filled their place. I now had Damien (who I met through work), Miguel, and Deshawn. Carlos got tired of the whole "casual" thing, although I'll never know why he would. I loved it! All three of my current men were fulfilling every need I had, financially and otherwise. I had money to actually live as opposed to just getting by. I could now afford to go out far more with my girls or by myself if I wanted to just have some me time. I purchased myself a whole new wardrobe, some jewels, and makeup. Before I knew it, I was walking down the street like J-Lo. (That's Jennifer Lopez for all you ancient non-millennials who are reading my book.) I was loving my new life and my new self!

As time went on, I became more of a risk-taker in regards to my casual dating. I would meet guys at bars sometimes, have them buy me a drink, and engage them in their pathetic conversation. Then when they asked for my number, I would act like I had somewhere to be and skedaddle. I got myself a lot free drinks that way. And I didn't just do it with drinks. I had guys take me out, pay for dinner, take me dancing or to the movies, you name it! Then I would conveniently lose their number. Sure, my method of operation was grimy and I didn't do it often, but it was useful when I craved a fun night out. The point is I would've never thought to do things like that or have the lady balls to do them as my previous whiny self.

This new "me" gave me self-confidence and a sense of freedom I had never experienced. It wasn't only useful for my liaisons with men or my nights out but with everything else in my life, too. My new confidence and centered sense of self allowed me to process stress better, complete tasks more efficiently, handle my pre-teen kids' attitudes easier. The old "me" would've lost my mind trying to raise three kids, but my new self was more of a boss, more grown up, and allowed me to deal with almost anything that came my way. Because I felt better about myself, my job was easier to handle, as well. Whenever I got into arguments or fights with people, they were easier to win because I loved myself more. Mind you, I was tough before, so imagine how tough I felt now!

Time went on, and I got to a point where I was casually juggling more guys. It became second nature to me. Almost all of them were well off financially and willing to help me with anything I needed. I soon found myself starting to manipulate and take advantage of numerous men just like my mother used to do. There was Juan, Alejandro, Jack, Gabriel, and Anthony. Oh, then there was Pedro and a hot Italian guy named Alessandro. Not to mention, the original trio – Deshawn, Miguel, and Damien – were still around, although Damien seemed to be moving on. Point blank, I had men throwing themselves at me, and I didn't hesitate to catch them and then throw them back once I'd gotten what I wanted. Nearly all of the guys who I was involved with were putty in my hands.

I felt so free – not just financially but sexually, as well. Before I'd never had a chance to explore my sexuality nor did I enjoy sex as much with my previous boyfriends and husband. I was much more in tune with my desires and couldn't believe I had been missing out all those years!

None of my guys cared that I wasn't serious as long as they were getting their pipes drained, and I didn't mind being the plumber since they were taking care of me. Upon hearing my longing to go out or to go shopping, they would hand over their credit cards to me. Since my taste became more expensive, I started adding men with bigger wallets into my circus act. Yep, I was getting carried away, but it was so damn easy. Thus, I was able to fulfill both my need for financial freedom and my need of a good sex life. And on my life went...another cock, another credit card...another cock, another credit card.

Not only did I benefit from these arrangements, but my children were more fulfilled, too. I was living a life where I was able to provide for them far more, and being that two of them were now teens, they were more costly and becoming more materialistic. All the time they spent with their peers going to movies and parties, hanging out and going shopping, buying beepers and new shoes, – all of those things required money! So, I was relieved I started my new life, because if I had stayed the old me, I would've been barely able to feed them, and they probably would've hated me for not being able to provide them with a comfortable life. Justin was still young, so he didn't need much. However, with prices rising, it was still getting expensive to take care of him, too. Therefore, I felt what I was doing with my men was definitely a smart move on my part. If I hadn't, there's a great possibility I would've been suicidal while trying to raise three children on my own. But, I digress. To put it simply, everything in my life came together at the right time and was balanced. Yep, I planned never to go back to the person I was before.

Chapter 33

Months went by. Parties went by. Money went by, and yes, cocks went by. I was having some of the best times of my life. I never had as much fun as I had within that last year and a half. I couldn't believe I had suppressed her my entire life – the Nina in the mirror. She was the real me! She should have been set loose upon mankind long ago, but I was too much of a pussy to let her out...too afraid of what might happen. But, it was all that ever needed to happen, because now I had total freedom.

    Mind you, it was still a headache raising three kids as a single parent, but not as much as before because I was making time to have fun. Before I was dead in the water, coming home to my kids stressed out and angry. Sure, my kids put a smile on my face, but my world revolved around them, which left little to no time for me to do anything for myself. But, I learned how to balance having children and a life of my own. A life where I had fun, got to hang out with my girlfriends, and was hit on by men left and right. A life where I could afford to go shopping and dine out. A life where I could go see a movie or drive to a cabin for the weekend and spend time with one of my men or by myself if I chose to do so. A life where I could afford a babysitter when I wanted to do any of those things. A life where I mattered because I was the center of attention and desired by many. No longer did my world only spin around my children. Yes, I love my kids more than anything in the world, but it felt amazing to have a separate life just for me. My life felt more complete; it felt more satisfying; it felt like I deserved it. I thought of it as my reward for having survived all that I had gone through.

In my opinion, that's the problem with so many families. Parents (or a parent) eventually become resentful, and as a result, they often try to hurt their kids or hurt one another because they don't have a fulfilling life. Everything they do is for the kids, the family, or the house. It's enough to make one feel like they are living a prison sentence. Stop acting like being married or having children means you can't be happy and have a life of your own! Very few people have a separate life from their spouse and kids, and that's why they eventually become resentful, which leads to the person either leaving, cheating, or even committing suicide. They don't allow themselves to have an outlet and remove themselves from the stress in their lives. I used to be like that, but now, I have the best of both worlds! You don't have to choose between having a family or having a life of your own. You can actually have both! *(GASP!)* Yes, you can actually have a life you enjoy with your kids and a life you enjoy for your motherfucking SELF!

One night, I decided to go out with Tania; we were meeting up with the girls at some club. Tania told me that she invited someone new to join us, though.

"So how have you been, girl?" she started as we sat on the bench waiting for a bus.

"I've been pretty good. Don't have much to complain about," I said, smiling.

"Yeah, I noticed." Tania laughed. "You've been different for a while now. Before, all you would do is whine, but now, you're always smiling and not complaining about nothing. What's going on, girl? Who got you smilin' so much?" she questioned, smirking.

I slightly laughed. "Nobody, girl, except me."

"Oh, really?" she responded sarcastically.

"Yep! I'm finally the one who's making myself smile, instead of depending on someone else to do it," I replied.

"Well, good! It's about time! That's how it should be," she stated.

"It took you long enough to figure that out."

"Better late than never!" I replied, and we both laughed.

"Listen, I'm proud of you. You deserve to be happy," she expressed solemnly.

"Thanks, mamacita. You're the best," I said, smiling and hugging her.

As we continued to wait for the bus, she said, "Hey, remember I told you that someone else is going to meet us there?"

"Yeah, you told me some guy would be joining us, right? Tell me about him," I told her.

"It's not just any guy. Umm, do you remember Dave?" she asked.

I started thinking. *Dave? Dave? Dave? Hmmm.* Then my memory lit on fire. Dave was an old classmate and childhood friend of mine. He always liked me, but I kept him as a friend. We saw each other here and there, talked occasionally, and hung out rarely but almost always among other company. We were never truly close, but he did know how I grew up. He knew about my family, my mother, my problems, a lot of the suffering I went through. He was a good listener, so I confided in him sometimes even though I had such a distrust of men. Because of that, I didn't let him get close, but he was still a good ear when I needed to vent. As I grew up, we drifted apart.

"Oh yeah, Dave! Holy shit, I haven't seen him in forever! He's coming?" I said, excited.

"Yeah, we stayed in touch up until I moved, and then he just dipset. But, I saw him in the market a little while back, and we got caught up. So, I told him we were going out and asked if he would like to join us," Tania said.

"Oh wow! Awesome! I'll be happy to see him. He was always a good dude," I told her.

"Yeah, and he still is," she said, laughing.

The bus finally came, and we were on our way to the bar. When we arrived, we met up with our girls inside. Then the fun began. Drinks, music, and dancing galore! An hour later, as Tania and I were laughing at the bar, I spotted a man walking towards us. Tania spotted him, too, and immediately stood up to embrace him in a hug.

"Dave! About time your ass showed up! How are you?" she said, smiling.

"Yeah, sorry. Got caught up in something. I'm good, though," he answered.

"Awesome! Dave, you remember Nina, right?" she said while turning to me.

Dave looked at me and lit up. "Of course! Nina! How you doing?" he said, then gave me the biggest, tightest hug.

"I'm good. Nice to see you again, Dave," I replied, smiling at him.

"Yeah, it's been a long time," he commented.

"Sure has," I agreed, smirking.

"Wow! You look amazing," he said, jovial and flirtatious.

"Thanks. You don't look too bad yourself."

Indeed, he was bigger than I remembered, a cool Irish/Italian mix, in his 30's, and handsome.

"Ha ha! Thanks," he replied.

"Anyway, let's order some more drinks now that you're finally here," Tania blurted out, breaking the romantic tension that was starting to arise between the both of us.

Fast forward to the end of the night. We all were drunk and laughing about bullshit. Needing some air, I stepped outside, and Dave followed behind me. We sat on a ledge and started talking.

"So how you been, Nina? What'chu been up to?" he asked with a warm smile.

Remembering again how good of a listener he was, I lovingly smiled back before dumping all my shit on him.

"Wow!" Dave responded, shocked beyond acceptance.

I pretty much told him everything that I'd been through.

"Holy shit! Nina, I never would've thought," he continued, slowly processing all the information. "Like how the hell did you wind up going through all that I'll never figure out. You were a real nice girl. I mean, I knew you had problems with your mom and all, but to think you– I mean, just wow!"

I laughed. "I know what you mean. Yeah, I tried to be the best person I could, but hey, sometimes that just ain't enough for life," I said sarcastically while smiling.

"Shit, I'll say," he replied, still shocked. "I can't say it was pleasant for me to hear, but I'm glad you told me everything," he added, laughing.

I laughed with him. "Yeah well, you were one of the few men in my life who was actually good to me and always listened to what I had to say. So, take it for what it is," I said, chuckling.

"I'm trying," he replied, laughing again.

After calming down, we shuffled between looking at the sky and at each other.

"So what about you? What's going on in your life?" I finally asked, breaking the silence.

"Hell, I don't think you wanna hear my story, hun, because after telling me yours, my shit will be the most boring thing you'll ever hear!" he stated.

I laughed.

"No, seriously, you'll fall asleep," he said with a chuckle.

"Hey, after telling you all of my bullshit, I think I've had my fill for tonight. I could use an average story to help me feel balanced. Trust me!" I told him, also chuckling.

He smirked. "Alright. Well, after school, I got a job in construction. I'm still working there, and I still live with my mother, helping to take care of her."

I looked at him, waiting for him to continue.

"That's it," he ended, chuckling.

I started laughing. "Wow, you weren't kidding," I said, then playfully hit him on the arm.

"No, I wasn't," he said, chuckling again.

That's when I stood up. "Well, we better get back in there before

Tania gets into a fight with the bartender or some shit," I said with a sigh.

Dave chuckled and started to follow me inside.

"Hey, Nina," he said, making me turn on the spot.

"Yeah?"

"Not to make this a date or anything, but you wanna have dinner with me next week?" he asked.

I smirked. "Oh, Dave, why are you lying to me? We both know that was intended to be a date."

He laughed. "So you haven't completely forgotten everything about me!" he remarked.

I smirked again. "The fact that you're a bad liar? No, I have not. And, yes, I'd love to go out to dinner with you. Now let's get back in there and find my homegirl before she breaks balls."

He chuckled while following me back in.

Chapter 34

A week later, Dave and I went out. A day after that, we slept together. Before he knew it, I had added him to my roster of boyfriends. I knew he wouldn't be as financially sound as the others with him taking care of his mom and all, but honestly, I didn't care about that with him. To my surprise, I didn't seek anything from Dave. I decided to be with him because he was actually a good guy, and I could tell he hadn't changed from how I remembered him. Mind you, I wasn't planning on putting everything to a halt and being exclusive with him, but I liked the fact that I could have someone to talk to when I needed and who would actually listen. Sure, I had Tania, but it was different with Dave. He always seemed emotionally supportive in a way others weren't; he would just listen without judgement or offering advice, which Tania didn't always do.

Life continued on, and I was living it up like I had been for a while. Deshawn sort of stopped seeing me after realizing I had been stringing him along for almost three years. I guess he understood I wasn't going to be serious with him. Most of the men I went out with were pretty much disposable; I would use them for what they were worth until they got tired and walked away. Hell, I couldn't get half of their names right, and by the time they left, it didn't matter anymore. I became colder towards men, and as time went on, I started viewing them more as objects instead of people. I'm not saying I strictly saw them as objects, but I I guess I just cared less and less for each one. I had my life, my children, and was having my fun. That's all that mattered to me. I felt free! But then…

Nina Garcia

One morning after getting out of bed, I threw up. Aww, shit! Well, you know what I had to do next. I was in the bathroom trying to pee, but it was hard to make myself go because I was nervous. Alas, the urine covered the stick that would soon play like a judge and render a verdict. Then I stood there waiting with baited breath. Aaaand...fuck! Yep, I was pregnant again. The clouds that I had been floating on evaporated, and I crashed back down to earth. I had been floating around for so long that I forgot what it felt like to be back on solid ground.

I was going to have another baby, and even though I could actually afford one now, I didn't want one! Three kids were enough for me. So, with a deep sigh, I made the decision to do what I thought I would never have to do again...have an abortion.

Don't get me wrong, I remembered my experiences with it in the past, but being a new person, I thought I would deal with it differently. So, I set the appointment and didn't tell anyone what was going on. The day came, and I had the procedure done. To my surprise, afterwards I didn't really feel depressed. In fact, I sat in the recovery room not feeling much of anything. Not depressed, not empty, nothing. This time was definitely different than before. Physically, I felt weak of course, but emotionally, I was indifferent about it.

I spent the next couple of days at home recovering. I didn't feel distressed like before when I had my previous abortions, and that fact didn't bother me. I actually felt great! I surmise that in being a new person, I was also far stronger than before. The emotional weight of this abortion felt as light as a feather, and I loved it! I loved not being a whiny bitch about it like I was in the past! I no longer had to be afraid of making tough decisions. If I was able to handle having an abortion – one of the toughest decisions for a human being ever – like it was an afternoon fart that took a long time to come out, I might as well consider myself invincible!

Chapter 35

Feeling indestructible, I got back out there and started meeting new people. With my last batch of boy toys dwindling down, I opened myself up to meeting a few guys and went out on dates. One guy named Blake wasn't into the whole casual thing, so he cut me loose when I told him I wasn't looking to settle down. Then there was Marcos, who I started seeing regularly, and David, some Jewish guy who immediately saw that I didn't want to get serious. However, he was okay with it oddly enough. While on a date with David, I recall him telling me with a smile, "You say you don't want anything serious now, but I'm sure I'll get you to change your mind. I don't expect a woman like you to be easy to keep." I thought to myself, *Okaaay*. His comment creeped me out a little, but because his pockets were deep, I just nodded as if there was a possibility. Now listen, I never set out to be a vindictive bitch, and I made sure to always let men know where I stood so my conscience could be clear. But, hey, if the guy didn't want to accept it, then it would be his problem when he got his arrogant heart broken, not mine.

Then I met Giancarlo a week later, but to my surprise, after a few dates and getting me into bed, he just stopped calling. I never got a dime out of him for anything. Honestly, I didn't expect that since I was used to most guys showering me with money, gifts, and trips. It never occurred to me that I might meet my match one day, someone who would do the same thing to me. I was surprised it didn't happen earlier, considering many men are known to play women just to get what they want and then never call them again. A lot of guys are great at being players, so the fact that I hadn't encountered one before Giancarlo was quite a surprise indeed. After Giancarlo, I realized how lucky I had been living my lifestyle for as long as I had and getting guys who stuck around and took care of me.

The man I met after Giancarlo was Roberto, who was from my background and had deep pockets. I was still seeing Dave, too.

In the midst of having fun, frolicking with guys who helped me financially, and taking care of my kids, I ended up getting pregnant again! And again, I wasn't thrilled, but this time, I wasn't scared of getting an abortion. No doubt I was absolutely going to get one. In fact, I was looking forward to confirming the strength of my new emotional armor. So, I got it done, and lo and behold, it didn't affect me! I was thrilled! I know that may sound cold, but don't get me wrong. I wasn't thrilled about getting the abortion, because it's not a good thing to do by any means. I was thrilled at my reaction to it – that I wasn't emotionally affected by it. And I moved on.

But, it didn't stop there. I continued seeing the men I had in my life, and it happened again. I got pregnant and had another abortion. Shit, I hoped this wasn't gonna be a regular occurrence. Sure, I had desensitized myself to having abortions, but it didn't mean I enjoyed going through it. I figured I just had to play it more safe. Didn't work. I got pregnant again, a few times actually, over the next couple of months...and yes, I aborted each one like I was taking an ibuprofen for a headache. I didn't even blink at the thought of getting an abortion...all courtesy of the "New Nina".

One day while cleaning around the house, I got a phone call.

"Hey," my mother said from on the other end of the line.

Holy shit! I had been so caught up in my new life that I didn't realize I hadn't talked to my mother in ages.

"Hey, Mom. What's good?" I asked, trying to sound welcoming, but it came off more regretful.

"Well, I wanted to know if you were still alive. I mean, I haven't heard from you in what, almost a few years now? And you don't come to see me or anything," she said, actually sounding worried.

"Sorry, Mom. I just got caught up with life and everything. My bad," I replied.

"You don't think I wanna see my new grandson? Are you trying to keep your kids away from me or something?" she asked.

Suddenly, I remembered why I hadn't reached out to her.

"Excuse me, but who the hell stopped you from visiting me? And while we're on the subject, how come I never heard from you? I ain't the only one with a goddamn phone! You could've called. You could've came over. And now that it's been a long time, you finally decide you wanna see your grandkids? You don't even care to say you wanna see me! Is that how it is?" I barked and then waited for her response, but I didn't hear anything except silence.

Then a slow, carefully plotted, and almost mournful reply fell from her lips. "I just...I didn't wanna bother you."

"Okay, well, you're bothering me now," I said in a comical kind of way, so as to make it seem like I was joking. I kinda wasn't, though. Well, maybe I was. I don't know. Fuck, was I?

Again hearing silence, I decided to break the ice.

"Look, I didn't really mean that, Mom, it was a joke, but still, why are you all of a sudden calling now after all this time and asking to see us? Why this moment?" I asked, trying to sound a little sorry for my brashness and somewhat inviting of dialogue.

I heard nothing but silence. I knew she didn't hang up, but the silence was bothering me because it went on for a while. Finally, I decided to try again before I hung up.

"Mom? Are you there?"

After a few seconds, she said, "It just started to get lonely here, that's all. But, sorry to bother you. Glad you're alive, and I'm glad the kids are okay."

Then she hung up. At first, I was kind of pissed that she said she was glad I was simply alive instead of at the very least saying she was glad to know I was doing well. No, the fact that I was alive was good enough for her. But then, I started thinking about the way she said that last line before hanging up, and it made me forget about the anger in an instant. I realized it was the closest to pain I'd ever heard in my mother's voice. It was barely there, and I wasn't even sure I heard it at first. It took me a little bit, but yeah, I'm almost positive I heard a hint of pain in her voice! Oh my God! How the hell did I hear it? She said the words almost the exact same way she usually said anything else – plain and cold. The slight difference was pain. I'm sure of it! Did I really hear pain in my mother's voice? No, I couldn't have. It didn't make sense. Not knowing what to make of it, I just shook my head in confusion and continued to clean.

My kids were hanging out with their friends for the night, and I had a date planned with Dave. After I finished cleaning, I started getting ready. As I primped in the bathroom mirror, something came over me. I stared at myself for a while, and then...I rushed to the toilet and threw up. When I went back to the mirror, I was crying my eyes out. The conversation I had with my mother earlier came rushing back into my consciousness, with all of its open messages and reflective themes. I sending me into a traumatizing shock.

"I'm just like her!" I started screaming to myself. "Oh my God! These past few years I have been living just like her! And now she's all alone! She has no one! She's going to die alone and in pain! She's lived like that her entire life, and now she is sitting in that fucking house alone and in pain! I didn't imagine what I heard! She was in pain! She's all alone and in fucking pain! And I'm going to end up just like her!"

The reality hit me like shots fired from a goddamn machine gun. I couldn't believe how stupid I'd been. All these years while living as the "New Nina", I was really living as my mother! And I would end up exactly like her down the road. The fear, the pain, the regret, the pity – all of it hit me hard! I fell to the floor, sobbing my eyes out. I don't think I've ever cried that much before. I became so disgusted with myself. After swearing to be different than the person I despised,

The Scars That Save Us

I still ended up here anyway, and ot hurt so fucking bad! I felt so wounded and was sure I would die there in my bathroom. It felt like my emotions were bleeding all over the floor. Like they were literally seeping out of every bullet wound, dripping down my body slowly, and covering the floor with pain and regret. I was shaking and threw up a couple more times. I continued sobbing until my phone rang.

It was Dave. He asked where I was, as he had waited for me at the restaurant before leaving and returning home. I looked at the time and saw that I was supposed to be there two hours ago. I'd been emotionally bleeding and crying in the bathroom for two fucking hours, and yet, it felt like forever. After wiping away my tears, I finished getting dressed and stormed out the door. I couldn't deal with it then. Truth was, I didn't know how.

*****

The two of us returned to the restaurant for dinner. I was still shook up during the car ride but managed to hide my emotions from Dave. After we arrived at the restaurant and went inside, we ordered our meal and started catching up. A minute into the conversation, I started getting shook up again and told him that I needed some air. I went out to the parking lot area in the back of the kitchen and threw up all over the concrete. I couldn't take it. I was so shook up from my earlier breakdown that I didn't know how I was going to make it through the date. There was so much to think about, so much to reflect on, and I didn't know if I wanted to do any of it. Then Dave came out.

"Nina, honey, are you alright? You've looked distraught the whole night. What's going on?" he asked, genuinely concerned.

His face showed so much warmth that it made me start to feel upset about how I had treated a lot of the men in my life. I started crying as he walked towards me.

"Hey, hey, it's okay," Dave said as he took me into his arms and hugged me. "Nina, why are you shaking? Baby, what's wrong?" he asked, hugging me tighter.

As we sat on a bench outside of the restaurant, I told him everything. I told him the truth about what I'd been doing for years – switching up guy after guy, having them help me financially, partying excessively, and basically using anyone I could for my benefit. I opened up completely, crying as I released a lot of leftover pain. My confession at least helped me to stop shaking.

Dave's reaction was surprisingly calm. He was shocked visibly but not in an over-the-top way. He reacted more sympathetically as though he was listening to a tragedy, which he pretty much was, and he was devastated for me.

"God, that made me feel so much better," I said, still wiping away tears.

"Good. I'm glad," he replied.

"I'm so sorry, Dave. I'm so sorry I dragged you into my life. It was never about the superficial bullshit with you," I told him, trying to sneak in a regretful tone in the hopes that he would be forgiving.

"I know that, Nina, but the fact that you were seeing other guys… I mean… You know what, forget it," he said. "It's all good. I'm not mad," he said, half-smiling.

"What?" I said, shocked out of my mind.

"I understand why you did it, so I ain't really mad. It's okay, babe," he said.

His casual responses made me feel even more confused, because I was certain he would be upset with me or at least disappointed.

"Are you serious? You're telling me you're not mad?"

He laughed. "Baby, you just explained to me in great detail why you were doing the things you did. I'm pretty sure I got the picture," he said with a chuckle.

I gave him a half-smile.

"Am I upset about the things you did and went through?" he continued. "Yes, but I ain't mad. Like I said, I kind of understand the headspace you were in. Besides, we never discussed being exclusive, so it's not like you were breaking a commitment with me," he said.

I was totally taken aback by his forgiving nature.

"Thank you so much for understanding!" I said through my tears.

"Yeah, of course. I mean, I'm glad you opened up to me, ya know. I'm proud of you. That took guts!"

"It was hard, but I'm glad I did it," I said, smiling. "So you wanna keep seeing each other?" I asked after a brief silence.

"Definitely," he responded with a chuckle. "And tell you what, I'm gonna keep helping you."

"Whoa! What do you mean?" I asked.

"Meaning that even though we're not serious and you have other guys who you're seeing or whatever, I'll still be there to help you financially whenever I can."

Confused and suspicious by his response, my eyes widened. "Dave, are you being for real right now?"

He chuckled again. "Yes, I'm being for real, Nina. I don't think it's fair everything you've had to go through in your life; you didn't deserve any of it. I know you're a single mom with three kids, so I will always be there to help you out in whatever way I can. I got you!" he said with a confident tone.

I looked at him as though he was my knight in shining armor. Then I started crying again, but this time from joy and not pain.

"Wow, Dave, you're amazing! You know that?" I voiced, while giving him a big hug. "I can't believe how amazing you are! Thank you!" I said with an overbearingly grateful tone and started kissing him.

He chuckled some more after I let him go. Then, after a brief pause, I laid out a question to him that I didn't think I would ask any of the men I'd been dating...

"Do you wanna get serious? Like just me and you exclusively, without any others in the mix."

He turned to me, paused for a moment, and then sighed. "I'm sorry, Nina, but I can't."

What?! I felt like I had got hit in the gut with a heavy basketball.

"Really?" I asked.

"I'm sorry, but I just don't wanna get serious with anyone right now. I'm good with the casual thing we got going on and would rather keep it like that," he responded in a sensitive tone.

What the hell?! Here we were, two childhood friends who caught up after many years and decided to start dating like it happens in so many romance movies that I've watched. He was one of the best men I've ever known and coincidentally the man who accepted me despite my flaws. The fact that he caught me in his arms and allowed me to vomit my pain onto him, while showing understanding and forgiveness, made me believe he was my knight in shining armor. I truly believed that because he ended up saving me, he would eventually want to get serious with me, and then the cinematic romance would culminate in me realizing he was the one for me. But this? He still didn't wanna be serious? What the fuck? I mean, I was shocked, but yeah, this was really happening. Holy shit, life, you cunning motherfucker! Reality, you twisted son of a bitch, you got me again! I sat there looking shocked for so long that Dave looked like he was about to take me to the hospital.

"Yeah, that's fine with me," I finally answered, nodding.

"Are you sure?" he asked with a chuckle, sounding unsure. "Seemed like you spaced out for a second."

I laughed. "Yeah, yeah, I'm good! Just processing a lot of stuff, but I completely understand. I'm fine with it," I replied while forcing myself to smile.

"I hope so," he said with a slight laugh. "C'mon, let's go eat," he finished, trying to comfort me with a jolly smile.

We went back inside to finish our date, and afterwards, he took me home. While in the bathroom stripping myself of my makeup and jewelry, I looked at myself in the mirror long and hard. That day was quite the revelation...and I came to one conclusion. I was done. I was finished. No more partying; no more dating men left and right and

The Scars That Save Us

using them; no more materialistically-driven motives and agendas; no more of my so-called "new life".

That's it!

What do you mean, that's it? What the fuck are you talking about, girl?

I'm talking about I'm done, sweetheart. I'm sorry, but this is over and done with.

But what about when you promised me that you're never going back? You said now that I was out, you were never going to push me back in! What happened to that?

What happened is that I'm not gonna end up like my mother. No way! I refuse!

Look, you don't know that you will!

Umm, sorry, but yes, I do! I know it will happen if I continue like this. I'm not planning on going back to the old Nina, mind you, but I don't wanna end up like my mother. So it's time for a change. Not a change back to my old self, just a change from this.

Are you sure you wanna do this? It took so much for you to let me out, so much heartbreak.

Yes, it did, and you're the vengeful manifestation of my heartbreak. You helped me, but now I want to let that heartbreak go. I want to let you go.

Are you sure? I mean, what if you still need me?

I'm sorry, girl, but yes, I'm sure. This is happening. I'm done.

But I thought I was the New Nina.

Well, sorry, sweetie, but I don't think you're new at all. You were always a part of me, but you're the part I don't want anymore, the part that resembles my mother to the core, and my past, and my pain, and all my heartbreak. You came at the time when I needed you, but I don't want to be reminded of all of that any longer. I want to let it go. I'm sorry, but I want to let you go.

Are you sure, baby girl?

Yes, I am.

And with that, I closed my eyes, opened them again, and was staring at myself. But I saw myself as myself and not any other version of me. The other Nina wasn't there anymore. I was now my old self, but I wouldn't be that Nina either. I wouldn't be either. Instead, I would be a new and improved Nina. Not one suffering from any heartbreak or loss, or one who was afraid. I would be a brand-new me that was at peace with myself instead of trying to form a new self... a stronger, more centered Nina. At the very least, I would be done with my serial dating. I would just keep taking care of my kids, my home, and maintaining my job. If I got into a serious relationship with someone down the road, maybe I would give it another shot, but for now, I needed to take a break and change my lifestyle.

I looked at myself in the mirror again, fearful but determined. Determined to start a new day and a new me...again...for the umpteenth fuckin' time. Oh Lord.

Chapter 36

The next day, I woke up, washed my face, and went jogging. When I got back home, I worked out for a bit and then made my kids lunch before they went to school. I decided to go to a gig to clean the house of some pop star. I wasn't planning to, but then I remembered I had to start changing my twisted life. The pop star ended up hiring me to clean for her on a consistent basis. I dropped most of the men I'd been seeing and focused on getting back into work mode. As he promised, Dave helped me out every now and then with my bills. The only guys I continued seeing were Marcos and Roberto, because they both really liked me and basically just stuck around. I tried to let them go, but they refused to be kicked out of my life. So, I still went out with them, although it was seldom. I wanted to concentrate on being at home more to tend to my house and my kids. I realized how much I'd missed out on time with Justin. He was growing up so damn fast, and I missed almost half of it because I was so into myself. Now I had a chance to spend more time raising him and getting to know him. He was such an amazing and happy little boy, always laughing and being cute. He was nothing like his dad, which made me see how grateful I should've been. My other two kids were still as punk as ever, but at least if I was home more, I could try to connect with them so as to avoid having them end up hating my guts like I did with my mother. I was reforming myself slowly, kind of like a hybrid of the old Nina and the new Nina. I found myself feeling lonely from time to time, but maybe that's what I deserved...to end up a lonely, old hoebag with a dozen cats!

One night, Tania called me to go out for drinks. I wasn't really in the mood, but since I hadn't gone out in a while, I decided to hell with it. I met up with her at our usual bar, where we ordered a few mojitos and started catching up. I ended up telling her everything, including me being promiscuous with men, my recent conversation with my mother, and how Dave rejected my idea of settling down with me. I have never seen her eyes grow so wide.

"WOW!" she replied.

"Yep, that's what it is, girl," I said while nodding at her in a deadpan kind of way.

"Holy shit! How come you never talked to me about any of this, girl?" she asked.

"Tania, did you pay attention to anything I said? I was living in an armored shell. I felt like I was living my best life! Why would I want to talk about my problems? I wanted to stop being the whiny bitch you always referred to me as being. Only recently did all this shit start catching up to me, and I didn't know how to process a lot of it," I answered.

"Well, yeah, I guess that makes sense," she replied.

"I'm glad you convinced me to come out. I needed this, girl," I told her.

"Yeah, I'll say. Now you know to listen to me more often," she said, chuckling.

"What are you talking about? I listen to you plenty," I said, smiling.

"Only the times when I force you to," she replied, and we both chuckled.

Then we took a break to sip on our drinks.

"So what now?" she started again.

"I don't really know. Just live life, I guess. Focus on raising my kids for now and all that," I replied.

"By yourself?" she asked.

"Well, yeah. I mean, I have Dave to help me out with any extra finances I may need, but in terms of raising my kids, I'm pretty much gonna be doing it full time besides working my housekeeping gig here and there," I said.

"Wow, I can't believe how amazing Dave turned out to be," she said angelically.

I sighed. "Yeah, I know. He's incredible. I would totally settle down with him, but like I said, he just wants it to be a causal thing with me, and there's nothing I can do about that," I answered in a regretful tone.

"I feel you, but still, you don't wanna try and get into a relationship and settle down with someone else? I mean, it'll be pretty hard to raise your kids the way you're doing now. What happens when they go to college and shit?" she asked.

"I feel you, girl. I don't know. I still have Marcos and Roberto around, but I don't know if I wanna be serious with either of them," I expressed.

"Why?" Tania asked.

"I ain't really attracted to them honestly," I admitted.

"Why?" she questioned.

"Well, Marcos is kind of a dick. He sleeps around with other girls besides me, and he wouldn't be a good father figure to my kids. So, I'm not entertaining the notion of being serious with him at all. As for Roberto, he's actually pretty sweet. He has money, takes good care of me, and I'm sure he would be a caring father, but I just... I don't know. I guess I'm just not really attracted to him like that," I said.

She chuckled. "So you're not *physically* attracted to him?"

"Sort of. I mean, not only physically. I just don't know if I'm attracted to the idea of being serious with him," I replied.

"Look, Nina, after everything you told me, I think you're just bullshitting right now! I mean, you obviously have a clear choice in front of you. Roberto sounds like a great guy. I feel you're trying to make excuses so you don't have to be in a serious relationship again," she said.

"Look, I ain't making excuses, alright! I just don't know if I'm attracted to the motherfucker, that's all"

She laughed. "That'll come with time, girl. You can't expect to have the whole package. But, it sounds to me like he has the important qualities that you need. I mean, he's a great provider, and he was competitive enough to stick around instead of getting scared away when you tried to get rid of him, right?"

"Yeah, pretty much," I answered.

"And he sounds like he would be good for your kids, too," she continued. "Isn't that what's most important?"

I thought about what she said for a second. "Yeah, you're actually right! He pretty much sounds like the best guy for me," I admitted.

"I'm telling you, you need to give him a chance! Try it and see how it works out," Tania said.

"Yeah, you're right, I guess," I responded.

"If you do, you gotta commit, girl. Don't just jump overboard at the first sign of the boat rocking. If you guys gel good, try to make it work, at least for your kids' sake! Think of how they're gonna look at you if they constantly see men coming in and out of your life like it's a revolving door," she said.

Again, she was right! This whole time, I didn't consider that my kids had been witnessing the wreck I'd been, and I shuddered at the thought of how it affected them.

"Absolutely, girl! Thanks a million! You may be a tough bitch, but you give me great advice sometimes and inspire me," I said with a smile.

"Yeah, I should be a fucking psychologist," she said sarcastically, and we both laughed.

"Really, though, thanks for always being there, Tania. I don't deserve a friend like you," I told her, getting a little misty-eyed.

"Oh, girl, you better not cry on me, because I will drop your ass in an instant since you don't deserve me," she said, and we both started to laugh through our tears.

"Thank you," I said while hugging her.

The Scars That Save Us

"You're welcome, girl," she said, hugging me back and smiling. "You know I always got you."

I returned home teary-eyed and filled with contentment. I really needed that time with my best friend. It felt so good to sit with her, just like old times, and have her give me some much-needed and welcomed advice, which I would take. I was going to give Roberto a chance. I really could use someone in my life and so could my kids. My attempts at having a healthy relationship may not have worked work out before, but guess what? I still picked myself up and moved on. And that's exactly what I would again if I had to. I decided I would give it my all. If it worked, then great. If it didn't, then I would move on. That's it. Roberto was a great guy who deserved a chance. Therefore, I would give it my best and try to make it work. Maybe, just maybe, it finally fucking would this time!

So, I abandoned Marcos–and my lifestyle in general–and decided to become serious with Roberto only. He was quite happy, as he always liked me. We started going out regularly and getting pretty close. He was from my culture, but he was warm, stable, and caring–unlike most of those fuckers! After a little while, I introduced him to my kids, and they took a shine to him, too.

Things were starting out pretty good, although I still didn't find myself that attracted to him. Don't get me wrong, it was better than before now that I had started getting emotions for him. However, it was pretty hard not to revert back to my old ways, especially when I would see guys who were way hotter than Roberto. I made it a point to fight my urges, though. I had to if I was going to change my life.

Chapter 37

After six months of dating seriously, Roberto and I decided to move in together. He proposed that we get a new place so everybody could live under the same roof comfortable, and he suggested we buy a house. I was a little conflicted with the idea. Yes, I was excited at the prospect of having my own house, but at the same time, I wasn't sure if I was ready for such a big move. However, I eventually came around to it, figuring it would be a good way to solidify my exclusiveness with him. My kids were excited, too.

So, he got us a house in the Bronx, and we all moved in together. And you know what? It didn't seem that scary once it happened. In fact, it actually brought Roberto and I closer since we were spending a lot more time together now. His relationship with my kids grew stronger, as well. He would drop them off to school every morning and help them with their homework from time to time. One day, I saw him sitting with Jessica helping her with a paper, and it warmed my heart. I felt like I could really trust him with my kids. He made it a point to be a good father figure to them, and I could tell he was genuine. Having him to help me take care of my kids was most important to me.

Since we were becoming closer, my attraction to him started to grow, and instead of just having decent sex, we actually started having great sex. (Well, it started being great sex for me. He had been living it up with my sexy, attractive self ever since we first started sleeping together.) Anyway, I started to feel a lot better about our relationship. I also noticed that I was becoming more emotional about things. It was slow, though. I mean, I couldn't expect my emotions to come back to me swiftly after having kept them suppressed for so long. I was slowly but surely becoming some of my old self again, and while it annoyed me a little that I wouldn't feel as confident or emotionally strong as I had in my "Sarah Conner/Harley Quinn" phase, I took solace in the fact that I would feel more content being the original me instead of a remix version. I was even more content that I would veer off the path of becoming my mother. So, for now, that was the plan. Become a slightly better version of my old self while making this new life with Roberto work!

Chapter 38

Over time, Roberto started to think about opening up a store. A hardware store. I couldn't figure out for what, as we were both financially sound and didn't need another source of income. But, he said it had always been a dream of his, so of course, I supported him. Months later, he leased a building and asked me to help him run the store until it got off the ground. I would have to leave my current job, which I was willing to do since I had worked cleaning houses long enough and was getting tired of it. So, we opened the store together.

He decided to stay at his current job and manage both his work and the store. *Oh great,* I thought. *Now he'll be gone most of the time and coming home late.* I remembered what that was like. Anyway, the store wasn't big and fancy, just a nice corner size. So, we didn't have to hire any extra help. We developed a system. Roberto would open the store in the morning and work the morning shift before going to his second job, and I would come in and work the rest of the day until close. It was just cashier work, which wasn't complicated. Roberto did all the unloading of product and stocking himself. The first few weeks weren't bad, mostly because they were slow and I barely had to deal with any customers. However, as time went on, it got busier.

Roberto was home a lot less, which meant we were spending a lot less time with each other. My kids were seeing us both a lot less now. This was becoming all too familiar to me. Yep, I was back in the married life, even though we didn't officially get married. I guess I sort of knew what to expect, but at the same time, I expected this relationship to be better. And in many ways it was since Roberto wasn't involved in drugs and gangs like my previous marriage. He was a good, hard-working man, not a STD-spreading psycho. The thing unpleasantly familiar was him barely being at home. But, everything can't always be great, so I took it as is. Hopefully, it would get better down the road, but for now, this was our sacrifice to make the store work.

Some days when Roberto came home, he would be so beat that he would just go straight to bed or fall asleep on the couch while watching television. He rarely spent any time with me, and let's not talk about our lack of sex. Since I was still detoxing more or less, I had to fight the urge of getting my needs met elsewhere. Yes, I still had the urge to cheat on him, and his indifference about having sex with me only made it harder to keep my promise of being a changed woman. Don't get me wrong, I didn't just want to have a superficial relationship with him. I would've been fine with him spending quality time with me, even if there was no sex involved. But, the problem was he wasn't giving me either! Honestly, he was becoming more like a ghost. Again, I'd lived this life before, but that didn't make it easier. It still hurt to feel neglected. I kept reminding myself that I just had to hang on until the store started doing well enough to the point where we could afford to hire help. Then we could spend less time there and more time together fucking like rabbits on cocaine.

Chapter 39

As we had hoped, business picked up with our store, and neither of us could handle it by ourselves anymore. So, when I asked Roberto to bring on some help, he got his friend, Ray, to come in and work with us. He mostly worked the shift with me, though, as the afternoon was usually busier than the morning, and Roberto liked to work alone on his shift. Ray mostly did the loading and stock work while I handled the customers and cash register. He was a nice guy, young, and eager to help. Roberto trusted him since he was a good friend and not some stranger. On the downside, since we had hired help, Roberto got lazier. For instance, sometimes he would ask me to open in the morning, or he would be so tired that he wouldn't be able to go into work at all. So, I would fill in for him. It wasn't enough that he STILL was barely ever home to spend time with us, but on top of that, he made me take on most of the work in the store! The funny thing is that since we had Ray to help, I actually (and naïvely) assumed we would spend more time together, but it turned out to be the opposite. He relied on Ray and me to handle the store most of the time while he either slept or worked at his other job.

I decided it was time for me to make my choice...a choice I didn't really want to make...a choice that was pretty much my last resort. I felt like I had no other options since he was barely home, and I was always stressed out from work. I didn't wanna do it, but I had to. It was time. So, I went and got...the Egg! Yes, the famous vibrating egg – the thing I kept hearing about that was responsible for saving many marriages! It was finally my turn to experience it. No, I didn't want to, mostly because I'm the kind of gal who prefers the natural experience with a real man, but like I said, I pretty much had no other options left.

While standing in front of the sex shop, I was nervous. I didin't know the rules of the perverted sex merchandise world, and I wondered how a lot of my friends went about buying their sex toys. They must've had no shame waltzing into a sleazy sex shop with guys who were already horny in there. Then I started to worry about someone seeing me.

Well then, why don't you go in quick before they do, you idiot? my inner voice yelled at me.

Quickly, I scuttled into the shop, and as soon as I walked through the doors, the cashier gave me a creepy stare while smiling.

Keep going, Nina. Pay him no mind, I told myself.

While walking down the aisles, I was bombarded by more horny stares from salivating men. Once I got to the aisle of dildos, a creepy guy came up to me and said hello, but I just ignored him. However, when I turned to look down another row, I felt him start to touch my ass. I got so creeped out that I pushed him into the wall and ran the hell up out of there! Needless to say, I didn't get what I had went there for. Instead, I made my purchase online, and five days later, I was a happier woman. Not sure why I didn't think of doing that before putting myself through a trip to a sex shop.

*****

As time went on, Ray and I continued handling the day and closing shifts, while Roberto opened the mornings but committed more to his other job and picking up the kids. It's kind of ironic that he wanted to open a hardware store because it was his dream, but then left Ray and me with the bulk of the responsibility of running it. Maybe he realized owning a hardware store wasn't all that he thought it would be and figured since I knew the business better than him, why not let me babysit it. The jackass!

Anyway, things in our personal life did not get any better. I wanted to spend time with Roberto and to feel like I had a husband (unofficial husband, of course), but it seemed like he didn't want to do anything with me anymore. Just work, help out with the kids, and then spend the rest of his time sleeping or watching TV. In my previous relationships/marriages, the attention-seeking was never this bad. Despite having the egg to satisfy me sexually, I still craved intimacy. To put it plainly, I missed having sex with a man.

At the store, Ray started talking to me more. I got the feeling he liked me, but he knew I was off limits. I was flattered with the attention he was giving me, though. I knew I wasn't going to do anything with him, but it felt nice. We talked and joked a lot during our downtime. The interaction with Ray was nice, but at the same time, I found myself suppressing the urge to jump onto another guy. So, while his company was flattering, I worried that it would be a little problematic in the long run.

I tried to make things work at home with Roberto. When he was home, I would try and do things to get him in the mood, whether it was buying lingerie, preparing a nice dinner for us, or even putting on some porn. I even tried giving him the supposedly never-failing blowjob from time to time. But, nothing was reciprocated. After a while, I tried to confront Roberto about our problems, but he brushed them off. He made it seem like we didn't have any and that I was overreacting. I tried my best to ignore it, figuring this was some phase and that it would hopefully get better. Oh, how naïve us little fuckers can be at times.

Chapter 40

One day, while I was counting the money after closing the store, Ray called me to the back, saying he was having a problem. When I went to the back, I looked over his product count.

"See, some of it isn't here," he told me.

I looked at it again. "Then you know what, just make a list of—"

I started but before I could finish my sentence I felt his lips on mine. Quickly, I pushed him away from me.

"Ray, what are you doing?" I said.

"I'm sorry, Nina," he replied, looking regretful. "I've just...I've just been crushing on you this whole time, and from the things you and I have talked about, I don't think it's right for Roberto not to appreciate you. I'm sorry, but I couldn't help it! I didn't plan on this happening. It's just that I was having a problem with the count, and then you came back here looking so beautiful. And I just–"

"Okay, okay, stop," I said, cutting him off. "Look, Ray, you're a great guy, and I'm very flattered that you have a crush on me. It's really sweet, but I can't do this with you. I'm with Roberto, and regardless of how he treats me, it doesn't give you the right to swoop in and make a move like that," I told him, speaking in a firm tone.

"I know. I know. It was impulsive, and I apologize. If you fire me, I'll understand completely," he said.

"I'm not going to fire you, Ray. Why would I do that? You're a sweet guy and a great help. I understand that you just got carried away, but like I said, I'm with Roberto, and the two of you are friends. So, nothing like that can happen again. Okay?" I told him.

"Of course," he said, nodding.

"Now, look, I'm tired. So, let's close up and get out of here. This will be our secret."

He nodded. Then we closed up the shop and left.

It took everything in me not to shove Ray's body against the wall and take his crotch in my hand, but I knew I couldn't. Not just because Ray was Roberto's friend, which could lead to a complicated, messy situation, but because I had pledged to start a new life. Yes, my relationship with Roberto was unfair. Yes, Ray was young, hot, and liked me. Yes, I had needs. But, still, I needed to keep trying with Roberto. I believed there was a spark left to light between us; it may just take more time to find it. Therefore, I couldn't cave in at the first sign of someone else being interested in me.

I knew it would be weird working at the store now because of the sexual tension between me and Ray, but I couldn't fire him for being a horny idiot. That wouldn't be right. Besides, knowing Roberto, he wouldn't hire someone new that he didn't know, and it took him a long time to get Ray because he probably had no one else to ask. So, if Ray were gone, the responsibilities of running the store would be solely on me, and God knows I needed the help. I would just have to deal with the tension at home and now at work, both of which I had not signed up for.

As time went on, things between Roberto and I did not get any better. He hadn't touched me in months and hadn't taken me out in forever. There was no eye contact, no compliments, not even an "I love you" shared between us. I know I promised myself that I would give it time, but how much time would I have to give? What if it was always going to be like that? Had he grown tired of me? Did he take me for granted and just think I would stay with him indefinitely despite how things were between us? Did he really think everything was okay between us now compared to what we had before? He seriously couldn't be that stupid or naïve! I don't know what it was, and I was done trying to talk to him about it because he wouldn't even do that! I didn't know what I wanted to do because he was great when it came to everything else. He was great with my kids, being more of a father to them than even their own; he was an amazing provider; and he was also a great person all things considered. I knew he wasn't cheating on me nor that he would, because let's be honest. If thousands of years of evolution and culture has taught us anything, it's that women KNOW when a man is cheating most of the time. So, honestly, I did not want to leave Roberto, but I didn't know how much longer I could handle his indifferent behavior towards me.

Chapter 41

One day, while closing at the store. Ray and I were putting the last of the equipment away. I caught him smiling at me in a friendly way, and just like that, I grabbed him, turned him around, and kissed him. He and I ended up having sex right there in the store. I know what you may be thinking of me, but I'm sorry. I tried to be reasonable, and I tried to be patient with Roberto. I tried my best to hang in there and be faithful, not giving up that easily like I had done with the others before him. I waited around, kept trying to make things work, but he obviously didn't give a shit about any of it. So, my bad if I stopped caring, too. Don't get me wrong, I had no intention of going back to being the charlatan that I was, but I decided I was going to enjoy myself with Ray until Roberto realized what an idiot he was ON HIS OWN.

After we did it for the first time that night, Ray was surprised I did what I did but was ecstatic at the fact that I finally reciprocated his hormonal love. Afterwards, I left without saying anything and went home. I wasn't going to leave my relationship with Roberto, but until he started to man up, I would have my little fling on the side with Ray.

The next day when I went into the store, I didn't say much to Ray outside of things pertaining work. After we closed the shop, though, I walked up to him and smiled. He smiled back. In that moment, we both realized what we were getting ourselves into. We gave each other a look that asked if we were fully ready, and when I read it in his eyes that he was game, I leaned in, and we locked lips again.

So, there it was! Ray and I started our affair...and life for me started to feel much better. I felt happier and didn't feel that guilty about cheating on Roberto. What I did feel sorry about is that he wasn't filling Ray's position. In truth, Roberto was the one I really wanted to be with. Yes, Ray was great, and I enjoyed being with him, but I wouldn't have even considered being with Ray if Roberto had cherished me more. So, Ray filled that void. He wasn't my new love or anything, but we did have our fun, though.

Every day, once work was done, our play began. I would have preferred to have sex with him in an actual bed. But, since we couldn't go to be each other's respective homes and hotels were too risky because we could get caught, the store was our best bet. Roberto wasn't home that much to notice whether I came home late or not.

After a while, it became a little uncomfortable always having sex in the backroom. So, Ray eventually purchased an inflatable mattress to put in the back. It was so cute. Almost every workday, we would close up, get a couple of beers and snacks from the deli, and get under the cover on our inflatable mattress. After making love, we would continue talking, laughing, drinking, and eating. Sometimes we would even watch something on the portable TV he brought with him. This went on for a few months, and on the weekends, I would mostly spend time with my son Justin and OCCASSIONALLY my other two children. Justin was the one who needed most of my attention since he was hitting puberty. As far as Roberto, I let him be. If he wanted to do something with me, then great, but he never did. It was my hope that eventually our relationship would get better so I could stop sleeping behind his back.

*****

One day, while Ray and I were at work, I got a phone call from my daughter, who sounded frantic.

"Mom! Quick! You gotta get out of there! Now!" she screamed.

"Hold up! Hold up! What's going on?" I asked, concerned.

"Mom, Roberto is driving to the store! He-he-he has a gun!" she started explaining frantically.

"Wait! Wait! What? Slow down. What happened?" I said, trying to calm her down.

"I don't know, Mom. I thought he went to work after opening the store, but instead, he came back home. He didn't know I was there, and he kept yelling while walking through the house. He was calling you names, calling you a bitch! Then I saw him take his gun out of the drawer. He said, 'I'll show her,' and then he stormed out," she blurted out.

My eyes widened.

"I just knew he was talking about coming for you! I don't know what you did to him, Mom, but you gotta come home now before he gets to the store!" she barked.

"Okay, okay, listen to me! Call your brother and tell him to pick up Justin from school and come home with him. In the meantime, pack you and your little brother's things. Jason will pack his things when he gets there. I'm on my way!" I told her and hung up.

No! This can't be! How the fuck did he find out about us? I made sure to turn the store cameras off every day! Okay, I don't have time to think about the how or why right now. I gotta get home to my kids.

After telling Ray what happened, we both left immediately – without closing or anything – and sped back home as fast as we could. I wasn't sure where the hell I would go, but I knew I had to leave with my kids. Ray suggested we go to his mother's house...in Maryland!

"Whaaaat!" I shouted.

Turning to me, he said, "It's the only way. He can find you everywhere else here. He knows where your mother lives, and since your accounts are joined, he'll know if we check into any hotel. So, the best thing for us to do right now is to go out of the state. We can lay low with my family until he cools off. He won't get to us there."

Even though it sounded insane to me, deep down I knew he was right. Shit, I couldn't believe it had came down to him and me running away together to Maryland. Fuuuuuck!

After pulling up and parking in front of my house, I blasted through the doors with Ray following close behind. My kids were so nervous and running around everywhere that they didn't even stop to ask who Ray was.

Jason came up to me. "Yo, Mom, what the hell is going on? I brought Justin back, and then Jessica is saying we gotta pack and shit!"

"Look, Jason, I don't have time to explain right now. All you need to know is that we have to leave NOW! So, please, pack your stuff – enough for a good while – and get in the car!" I said, using a tone that let him know it was THAT kind of bullshit...the kind of bullshit his mother was very good at getting into.

Obeying me, Jason quickly started packing whatever he could, as did Jessica. But then, I checked the camera on my phone and saw that Roberto had already been to the store, saw we weren't there, and left to come back home.

"Okay, guys, enough packing. We gotta go NOW!" I screamed, then scuttled them out of the door.

Ray went to start the car and opened the doors for them.

"Wait! Hold up!" Jessica said.

"WHAT?" I yelled, then watched as she ran into the bathroom to get all of their toothbrushes.

For real? Why in such a dire situation as ours did she feel it was so important to risk our lives for a hygiene product?

Anyway, my daughter made her way into the car with my sons. Then I jumped in, and we burned out of there. I was so relieved that Roberto hadn't made it back before we left. I had no idea how he found out about me and Ray, but obviously, he was not in his right frame of mind if he was armed with a gun and hunting for us. No, he was more like a Puerto-Rican Wolverine who had just got his balls whacked hard and was on an uncontrollable tantrum. Ray was right. There was no way we could stay there in town. We would have to lay low at his mother's house...in motherfucking Maryland! Oh, Lord!

Chapter 42

While we were on the road, I told my kids everything that happened, and they weren't too thrilled. I think they were more irritated with the fact that they had to pack up and move quickly than they were with any of the drama that transpired with me. I mean, we woke up that morning thinking it was going to be a regular day like any other. Then next thing, we were running for our lives from my psychotic boyfriend, driving to another state with my lover who they had just found out about, and we would be staying with his family who I knew nothing about for God knows how long! I had no idea what I would do about my children being in school. If they didn't show up for a while, they would eventually get expelled. Then there was Roberto, who might get the cops involved to try and track me down. I could just imagine him making up some story about me having done something illegal just so he could get me hemmed up. For all I knew, we might have to live the rest of our lives as potential fugitives.

Good going, Nina. Don't be surprised if your kids end up signing into an orphanage themselves after this, and I won't blame them either. Sigh.

Anyway, we finally arrived at his mother's. We were all dead tired. While en route to Maryland, Ray had told his mother what had happened and that we would need to stay there for a bit. He didn't go into details. He just told a little white lie, saying he worked with me at the store, and after Roberto and I had a fight, he went crazy and came to the store with a gun, and therefore, we needed to flee. I expected her to give me a bitchy welcome after what she heard, but it was actually the opposite. She turned out to be warm and sweet. As soon as we came in, she welcomed me and offered us some dinner, which I declined, saying we were all just exhausted and wanted to go to bed. She understood and led us to a few bedrooms. As I got the kids ready for bed, Ray went back out to the car to bring everything into the house. His mother gave me some fresh washcloths and towels. After washing the kids and putting them into bed, I tried to wait up for Ray in the second bedroom but ended up falling asleep myself.

During breakfast the next morning, Ray and I started running down the events in detail that led up to us arriving on his mother's doorstep. He spoke about our affair, stating that was the reason why Roberto chased us out of town. His mother was definitely shocked about everything, but to my surprise, she was more sympathetic than judgmental. Ray explained to her that it wasn't right for us to be having an affair, but it was just one of those things that happened. Like I said, she was pretty understanding. She told us that we were more than welcome to stay there for as long as we needed. Ray seemed to be blessed with a great mother, and I found myself silently wishing I had the same type of mother while growing up. Their house seemed different, too. It was more homey and suburban than anything that I came from, and I grew up in a suburban house! I guess because it was Maryland, the people and the lifestyle were different. I liked it way more!

Ray's father was away and would return home in a few days. His mother told us that she had already informed him of what was going on.

After breakfast, we unpacked and got settled in. I decided to call my children's school and let them know we had to leave town due to an emergency and would be back soon. I was still nervous, though, because I had no idea when we would be able to return to New York. And what about Roberto, my crazy ex-boyfriend? (I think it's pretty obvious we were broken up now.)

As my kids and I started adjusting to life in Maryland, we went sightseeing and met more of Ray's family. His father returned home a few days later, but Ray and his mother decided not to tell him the whole story. They just told him that I was his new girlfriend and was staying temporarily. He was fine with it. Much like Ray's mother, his dad was pretty mellow and minded his own business. They had a pool, so my kids had the chance to swim and have some fun. We even had a barbecue with a lot of his family attended. All in all, we were having a good time. They all liked me, and it was refreshing to be in a totally new environment amongst new people. I started wishing I could stay there, but I knew that was highly unlikely. So, I decided just to enjoy my time there as much as I could while it lasted.

    I still thought about Roberto, though. It was strange that even after what he did, I still worried about him and wondered if he was alright. Who knew what mental state he was after everything that happened. For all I knew, he could've been deep in a depression or even worse, suicidal. The fact that he had a gun in the house made me even more nervous for him. I tried to distract myself so I wouldn't think about him, but the thoughts still lingered in the back of my mind.

Chapter 43

A few weeks later, I received a letter at Ray's mother's house that was addressed to me. It was from the NYPD.

They know I'm here! Fuck me! But how?

When I opened the letter, it felt like my stomach hit my mouth. Apparently, the van that Ray and I drove off in that day to escape was registered under Roberto's name! He claimed it was stolen, and the letter was ordering us to return the vehicle immediately. I guess they tracked us to Maryland through the van. Great! Now I was faced with making the decision to either go back to New York and potentially get murdered, or refuse the request and become a fugitive. Either way, I was fucked!

That night, Ray and I mulled things over. I had no idea what to do and neither did he. We both were panicking. I was sitting on the couch, and he was pacing around the room. I finally decided to go back. I told Ray that if I didn't, they might come after me there, and I didn't want to bring my mess to his parents doorstep. He wasn't happy about it, but he understood.

The next day, the kids and I packed our things and started on our journey back to our hellhole to face the mess I created. Ray expressed his love me and said he wanted to be with me after everything was resolved, but I told him it wasn't going to happen. He was kind of devastated by my response, but I got him to understand that him and I being together would never work for me. I'm sure deep down he knew what we did was a mistake and never should've happened. Just a few years ago, I finally had as close to a good life as I ever did – with a great man, my kids, a house, and a job. Then, it all went to shit. Yes, I was to blame, but so was Roberto! After all, I tried working things out with him, but nothing worked. And it kept not working until finally I was pushed into Ray's arms! Still, I couldn't try and justify my actions. I had fucked up, and now it was time for me to own up to my mistake.

*****

We came back to the city, and I made my way to my mother's house. I hadn't been this nervous in a long time. Luckily, Roberto hadn't said anything to her. So, I told my mother everything that happened and that we would need to stay with her for a few days. She actually seemed like she missed me and the kids, but I know that was more because she was lonely and not because she really cared about us. Still, I was not planning on staying there indefinitely.

The next day, I went to the police with the van and the letter, and I decided to tell them everything that happened. I told them about how Roberto wanted to kill me and how I feared for my life and the life of my kids. Surprisingly, the police were understanding, and in the end, they decided that I could go back and stay with my mother while they conducted an investigation. Of course, I had to leave the van with them so they could notify Roberto that he could pick it up. I was so relieved because I thought for sure they were going to keep me in custody since Roberto had reported that I stole the van, or even worse, they would force me to go back home to him. However, since Roberto wasn't legally my husband. I guess that worked in my favor, which resulted in them being lenient and allowing me to walk out of there. I was freakin' relieved, man. All that was left to do now was to arrange with Tania to go to her place tomorrow and stay for the time being.

By the time I got back to my mother's, my kids were still in school. My mother and my brother weren't home. Since I was alone, I figured it would be a good time to get some rest. I had been put through the wringer for the past twenty-four hours and desperately needed to get some sleep and clear my head.

Minutes after lying down on the couch, I started to slip away...slip between montages of the past few years. Flashes of Roberto and us living together...him doing homework with Jessica, and playing basketball with Jason...us cooking together after we first moved in together. The times when we laughed, danced, cried, and just lived life together. Then my memories grew dark as I thought about him sinking between the cushions of the couch as he watched TV while holding a third bottle of beer in hand. Flashes of me doing homework with Justin on a Friday night while no one else was home...flashes of my affair with Ray, the two of us laughing together while at work, lying on the mattress in the back after making love, and just talking and joking around. Then there were the thoughts of us driving off to Maryland while constantly checking the rearview mirror to see if Roberto was chasing us on the road.

The ringing of my phone woke me up. I must have slept for hours, and the house was still empty. I looked at my ringing phone, and my eyes widened. It was Roberto. I kept looking at it, thinking if I should answer or not. I decided to pick it up.

"Hello," I said.

"It was wise of you to bring my van back," Roberto said in a rather easy tone from the other end.

My heart started beating fast. "Look, Roberto—"

"Where are you now?" he asked, cutting me off.

"I'm sorry, Roberto, but I won't tell you that," I responded firmly.

"Okay, fine, but do you have time wherever you are?" he asked.

I was a little confused. "Time for what?" I asked.

"Time to meet up," he said.

"For what?" I inquired.

"Just to talk," he told me.

"Oh, really?" I replied suspiciously and sarcastically.

"Look, I'm not upset anymore, alright? What's done is done. I'm just glad you're safe, and if you're free, I wanna meet up with you so we can talk things out, that's all. We can meet in a public place. Can you come down to the park by our house?"

I could actually hear sincerity in his tone – the same tone he had when we first started going out, the one with warmth and soul, not the cold one he started to develop after a while of living with me.

I thought about it for a moment and finally said, "Okay, I think I can do that."

"Okay, good. I'm closing the store in a half-hour, so I'll go there afterwards," he told me.

"Okay, I'll meet you there," I said, then sighed as I hung up.

I wasn't sure what I was getting myself into or what would happen at the park, but what I did know was that I was tired of running and hiding.

Chapter 44

Sitting on a bench, I waited for Roberto in the park. After a short while, I saw him strolling towards me. He came up and sat down next to me. He didn't hug me or anything, which was fine with me because that's how I wanted it. As we sat there next to each other in silence, Roberto looked over at me a couple times, and I looked back at him. Neither of us really knew what to expect from this. Last we left off, I was trying to escape his attempt on my life when he found out I was having an affair. That day, he ended up losing me, the kids, and a store employee. Needless to say, both of us were more than a little agitated and jittery at the sight of each other for the first time in weeks. After a few minutes of silence, Roberto sighed.

"So how you been?" he started.

I looked at him. "Not bad, considering I would've been killed two weeks ago if it wasn't for my daughter," I responded, throwing a low blow.

He smiled slightly. "Yeah, sorry about that," he said, sounding a bit regretful but in a nonchalant way.

"Sorry?!" I snapped. "That's it? Sorry? That's all I get after being chased out of town by you!" I continued.

"Now, hold up. First off, who's to say I would've pulled the gun on you, Nina? I was pissed off and acting on impulse, but do you really think I would've gone as far as to murder you once I got there?"

I squinted at him. "Umm, why the fuck did you race to the store with a gun then, idiot? What, were you trying to scare us and then laugh after you pulled a blank and we shitted our pants? Were you trying to be funny? Was that your reaction to finding out about Ray and me, turn into a fuckin' comedian and try to scare us out of the affair? What exactly was your intention, Rob?" I snapped, being super sarcastic.

He laughed while looking uncomfortable and embarrassed. "Okay, okay, I deserved that. I won't lie. Yeah, I was pretty pissed off, and honestly, I didn't know what I was gonna do. I was just acting on my emotions," he confessed.

"Yeah, well, let's just hope your emotions don't end up with you actually killing someone next time," I said, using sarcasm again.

"Hey! Enough with the bullshit! Let's not forget what you did to me, alright!" he snapped back.

"Yes, I did cheat on you, Rob, and I'm sorry! I know it was wrong! But you gotta understand, you're the one who drove me to do it. Don't you get that! You didn't make it easy for me to remain faithful to you when you wouldn't even touch me, never spent time with me, and were barely home. When I tried to talk to you about it, you brushed me off like my feelings didn't matter! Do you remember all of that, Rob?"

He looked away from me and sighed. "Yeah, I do," he muttered, sounding even more regretful.

"So there you go! I didn't wanna do what I did, believe me. Hell, if you didn't hire your hot friend to work with my ass alone in the store, I probably would've never done it. It's not like I was going out after work and looking to have an affair with somebody. However, because he was right there, and he liked me, and we were always alone with no one but each other to talk to and laugh with, it just happened! It didn't happen for the longest time, though. I tried to deflect the attraction, to stop him and me from hooking up! I kept trying to spice things up with you, but nothing! Nothing ever happened between us! What was there to protect if it felt like we didn't even have a relationship anymore? We were like two strangers living in the same house!" I snapped.

"So that's it? The sex? That was the problem this whole time?" he asked sarcastically.

"No, you idiot, sex wasn't the only problem! Yes, it was an issue, but I tried to handle it without you. I got myself a fucking egg!"

Roberto smirked. "Yeah, I found that thing in your closet."

"Anyway," I continued, ignoring his comment, "the point is I would've been able to deal with the fact that we weren't having sex if you had compensated for that by either spending time with me, taking me out, or planning a vacation with me and the kids. As long as I got attention from you and wasn't left to feel like I was alone, I would've gotten by with the lack of sex. But, I didn't get anything from you! Nothing! So you tell me what you would've done if the roles were reversed?" I finished.

"Look, I get it! I'm not defending my indifference in our relationship. To be honest with you, I knew it was coming. I wasn't blind to the problems that were going on between us. I just pretended to be," he admitted.

"Why?" I asked, confused and upset.

"I guess because I didn't wanna deal with it. I was going through so much with work and the store. Then, having to work on our relationship on top of all that, I guess it was just too much. I just figured we could wait it out until–"

"Until I slept with someone else!" I interjected.

He put his head down again. "Like I said, I'm not defending myself. I knew it was bound to happen, but it still angered me when I found out," he said with regret in his voice.

"So why didn't you choose to DO something about it then to prevent it from happening?" I barked.

"It wasn't that I didn't wanna deal with it. I didn't really know how to," he said.

"What?" I replied, confused.

He sighed. "Nina, I never told you this, but you were my first real relationship. I had women before you, of course, but they were short-term relationships. You were the first woman I lived with, took care of kids with, and started a life with. I ain't ever been married or lived together with any woman. So, it was all new to me, and I didn't have the experience or wisdom to know how to navigate things," he confessed.

"Wait. What?" I said, shocked.

"Yeah, you were the first woman I fell in love with, and I figured once I got you, I had you. It didn't occur to me that I had to put in effort to keep us together. I just thought this was what it was," he told me.

I couldn't believe it. Roberto was pretty much in the same place I was when I got married the first time. Just like me, he didn't know how to put in the needed effort or what methods to use to navigate the relationship. He just hoped things would work themselves out...the same way I did when I was going through my shitty marriage with Pito. Suddenly, I felt sympathetic towards him.

"Wow, Rob, I wish you would've told me this. I would've tried to help you to navigate our relationship better. If we talked about it, I could've told you what to do more, how to deal, or we could've went to couples counseling. I mean, I did try to talk to you about things, but if I would've known where you were at mentally, I would've tried harder," I told him.

"I know, Nina. I just didn't wanna admit anything; I wanted to always brush things off. It was the only way I knew how to handle things. I didn't wanna admit that I didn't how to solve our problems. I ain't talking about the sex, but just the fact that we were never in the right time. When you were blowing me and shit, I wasn't in the mood because it wasn't the right time. I would always have something happen to me at work or some shit with my boss that day, and I just wanted to unwind and not do much. Trying to balance everything from work, to you, to kids – I just didn't know how to navigate it all, and I didn't wanna admit it," he said.

"But the truth is, you were the only woman I ever truly loved," Roberto continued. "Even when you were away these past weeks, I always thought about you – if you were okay, if the kids were okay. I was constantly worried about you. I didn't come after you, though, because I wanted to give you space. I knew Ray would keep you safe. He's a good guy. I've known him for a long time. The only reason I reported my van stolen is because I needed that shit back," he said with a chuckle.

I smiled. "I love you, too, Roberto. I truly do. More than I thought I ever would."

He smiled back. "So can we move on from this? Can you come back to me?" he asked nervously.

"I'll have to think about it," I responded with a smile.

He sighed. "You always like to tease, don't you?" he said, smirking.

"It's not just that, Rob. I got my kids to think about, too. I mean, they knew you were coming after me with a gun in hand, and they were afraid you were gonna kill me! I don't know how they'll be if we just move back in with you, so I gotta talk it over with them first," I explained.

"Yeah, you're right. I got you," he replied.

"But I do have to say, you were always an amazing dad to them, and I'll always be grateful for that," I said, smiling.

"Hopefully, they still remember that when you speak to them," he said.

"I'm sure they remember," I told him, smiling again.

We sat in silence for a few seconds – him with his head down, and me, sighing and looking around. Then he lifted his head up and smirked.

"You gotta admit, I was one crazy motherfucker, huh? Trying to hunt you down with a gun. I still can't believe I did that shit! Pretty funny, huh?" he said, laughing awkwardly.

I guess he thought if he gave a comedic edge to our incident, it would make the memory better. But, I just squinted at him like the dumbass he was.

"Yeah, hilarious! You should include that in a standup skit at a club sometime, idiot!" I barked annoyingly while he kept awkwardly laughing at himself.

"I'm just saying, someday we can look back on this and laugh," he said, nervously smiling at me.

I squinted at him again.

"Okay, okay, some very far off day," he said, chuckling as I sighed at his stupidity, shook my head at him, and turned back to the horizon.

We both sat in silence for a bit.

"I truly am sorry, Nina...about everything," he expressed, and I could tell it was genuine.

"I know you are, Rob. Now I gotta go," I said, getting up.

He got up and hugged me goodbye.

"I'm glad to see you again," he said, smiling.

"Me too," I said, smiling back.

Chapter 45

I walked back home rather relieved. Having that conversation and having Roberto open up about everything made me feel a lot better, even if I wasn't sure that I would go back to him. Still, what he did had scared me and shattered my trust for him. Besides, who knows how my kids felt about Roberto now after seeing that side of him. But, I was also surprised at how normal and calm our conversation was between us. I mean, every time I had a falling out or went through some crazy bullshit with a man, most times it was followed by some insane, traumatic experience. Each collision with an asshole somehow created a black hole in its place that almost swallowed me whole. So, to be able to communicate with Roberto in a civil manner was quite a change of tone. I appreciated it but was a little suspicious, not fully believing it really happened like that. Although to be fair, I did experience a crazy incident with Roberto when he forced me to run for my life all the way to fuckin' Maryland!

Now that I think about it, maybe this is just what happens afterwards. Maybe after two people deal with being pushed to the brink of insanity or experiencing a traumatic incident that tears them apart, they just have to make a return trip to earth, pick up the rubble, and confront the scars. It seems to me that's when the mature talk and forgiveness begins. So before, if all my relationships ended like the apocalypse, maybe this was now heaven. Life after the apocalypse…the point where you and your partner come back to each other as different people. The only other person I achieved that with was Pito, when he came back to me after serving time. However, he wasn't a different person when he came back. He was the same shmuck he had always been or maybe worse. But, with Roberto, this was truly a reunion with renewed eyes. We came back to each other more mature, more wise, and more open to talking things out instead of running away from or burying the problem. Maybe we had finally reached the point where we could have a mature, adult relationship. After many years of trying in our separate lives and then trying together, we finally got there...and it almost took a fatality to get to a rebirth.

Once home, I went into my bathroom, you know, for some more monologue and self-reflection. I stared into the mirror at my reflection, processing everything. I could tell Roberto loved me, and strangely enough, I still loved him. Even after everything that happened, after feeling so neglected, after having an affair and then being chased out of town by him – for some reason, I came to terms with how much I still loved him. It was strange, or so very strange. Even when I was married to Pito, I never felt for him the way I felt for Rob. To be honest, I mostly married Pito so I could free myself from my mother. However, being married to someone usually helps you develop feelings for them, which it did with Pito somewhat but not as much as with Roberto. Despite not being married to Roberto, I still somehow felt more genuine love for him than I did my children's father. With Roberto, I never stopped loving him, even after our apocalypse...even after our end of days. It was so strange, and yet, I had trouble accepting it.

I mean how could this be? There was really nothing special that happened with Roberto. No butterflies or spark in the beginning. No romantic opening to our relationship. Just casual dating, and yet, he ended up being the one I loved the most.

It's not possible, I kept thinking to myself. *This is not how things work.*

All my life, I grew up hearing and watching how true love relationships happen. Falling in love with your childhood friend and

The Scars That Save Us

then realizing your feelings for each other halfway through life; meeting the right person in some crazy situation and realizing you're meant to be; a fateful meeting with someone and a whirlwind romance evolves that leads to a happily ever after; or a fateful encounter followed by a falling out, only for the two people to reconnect years later and realize fate brought them back together. Yada, yada, yada, but short story, that's what I dreamed of and always wanted. Yet, the "romance stories" in my life always ended up in failure! Why? This wasn't supposed to be! I wanted my romantic story with the happily ever after. THAT'S what I wanted!

As I stared at myself in the mirror, I got teary-eyed. Then after analyzing my pathetic life, it all hit me at once, and I started breaking down.

"I WANT MY ROMANTIC STORY!" I started screaming while banging on the mirror. "GIVE ME MY ROMANTIC STORY BACK! I WANT MY ROMANTIC STORY BACK!"

I continued to bash on the mirror while crying my eyes out.

"IT'S NOT FAIR! WHY DO SO MANY GET ONE AND I DON'T? I WANT MY ROMANTIC STORY BACK! THIS IS NOT HOW IT WAS SUPPOSED TO BE! THIS ISN'T FAIR! I WANT MY ROMANTIC STORY! I DESERVE MY ROMANTIC STORY! GIVE IT BACK TO ME! GIVE IT BACK!"

I kept yelling and banging the mirror while sobbing, but I knew it was no use. The mirror wasn't listening. The universe wasn't listening. No one was listening. Maybe this was life's ultimate trick...for me not to ever fall in love, or should I say for me to fall in love but have my dreams crushed and fantasies diminished in the end.

Sobbing uncontrollably, I sunk to the floor. I dreamed of having my princess moment, where I would live with an honorable knight who swept me off my feet. Yet, here I was fighting feelings that were bubbling up for a man who I never thought I'd have feelings for. Why, after everything I went through, did I not deserve a fantasy to come true? I mean, this whole time, instead of looking for real love, was I just looking for the prettiest package it came in? Why did I have fantasy-like romance stories before that ended up in failure, and then when I found real love, I hated the way I found it? I never understood why life does that – give you fantasy versions of the things you want and then the honest versions later. Or why parents give us pretty answers first and then truthful ones later. It's like most of the time, everything you experience is nothing but a sugar-coated version of what the end product will be. But then, I thought about why I raised my kids in a similar way, covering them in a bubble when they were young so when the time came for them to face the subconscious trauma placed in them by their parents' failures, they would be ready for it. And when they faced the world, it would be easier for them to have a conversation with it, because the world rarely talks nice.

I smiled to myself because it was right then that I finally understood life's endgame. I realized that maybe life gives us romantic and sugar-coated versions of experiences in the beginning just to ease us into what the real thing will be. Maybe it just wants to make sure we're ready for the real thing, so it needs to give us a few practice runs first – practice runs that come in the package we like, the package that will attract us so we can enter those practice runs. I mean, you won't really buy something if it doesn't look nice, right? So maybe life has to give us its lessons in pretty wrapped packages that it knows we'll accept because we think there's something sweet within. That'll be the only way it'll get us to accept the lessons we need – through pretty packaging like all my romance stories came in, huh? So, maybe that means Life and Reality–those two annoying siblings–actually do care for us little nuggets at the end of the day, and they just need to set us up in their twisted games so we can be ready for the real thing when we're finally faced with it. Well, if that's true, then maybe, just maybe, they aren't truly assholes after all, eh? But, what the hell do I know? Well, I know if I didn't have my test runs with my previous relationships, I probably would not have known what to do with Roberto, the one who ended up being the love of my life.

Anyway, after crying until I could cry no more, I finally admitted my feelings towards Roberto to myself and decided I would get back with him.

Epilogue

After having a talk with my kids and them agreeing to it, we moved back in with Roberto. Since they still loved him as a dad, we tried again to be a family, but after a few years, it ended. We descended into the same problems as before, with lack of attention, and decided to break it off. After that, I decided to take a long break from relationships, maybe an indefinite break.

I decided to go back to school and get my GED. Then I started a career as a nurse. Wanting a fresh start, I ended up moving to Connecticut with my children, where the standard of living was better and the rent cheaper. I got myself a nice house and had a good career. My mother moved to Connecticut, also, to be closer to me. And my brother? I guess he left home to be on his own. Although I could swear I saw him around time to time when I was back in the city, wandering around still with the old bulge in his pants. I wasn't sure if it was really him though or if my mind was playing tricks on me.

While working as a nurse, I raised my children until they went off on their own. My son, Jason, finished college, and then moved in with his girlfriend. They now have their own kids. My daughter got her GED, moved in with a guy, and has a son now. And my youngest, Justin (yeah, the Spawn of Frankenstein) finished college and ended up getting married.

One night, I was arrested for a DUI, and my nursing license was revoked. (I swear I had like 0.2 percent alcohol in me, those motherfuckers!) So, I had to get a new career. I decided to get into real estate and started studying for my license...and Dave was still there to help me like he said he would. Anytime I needed help with finances or even paying a small monthly bill, he was always there. Didn't matter if I hadn't called him in months. Whenever I needed his help, he would send me a check without any hesitation. He really was one of the best men I've ever known. Bless his too-good-to-be-true soul!

I've continued on with life – living in my house, studying for a new career, being single and independent...and my life is better than it has ever been! It's not the best life, or amazing, or romantic. It's just better. And you know something, I think that's how it turns out for everyone really. Even though most people always seek out the happy fairytale ending, for the rest of us naïve little fuckers, life simply just ends up being BETTER! That's it, people! Not amazing or incredible. Not some rags-to-riches story that culminates in vast wealth or success. Not a fairytale with a happily-ever-after ending. Just simply better than it was before! That's the way it ends up for most people.

At least, that's how my life ended up. It still sucks. It's still depressing. It still bombards me with crazy obstacles from time to time and loads of stress all the time, but you know what? It's BETTER than it was before! That's how things ended up for me. Not romantic, not sensationalized, and not rags-to-riches cinema. It just ended up motherfuckin' better! And that, my friends, is life's ultimate twist – the one it plays on everyone. The twist that most of the time just ends up getting a little better instead of being all the romanticized outcomes you expect. And you know what? I think that's what anyone should hope for really.

So, now that this fucked-up but strangely charming story is over, go ahead and close the cover and put this book down. You're probably going to throw it on a shelf where it'll gather dust, but that's okay. Maybe you'll remember the messages I tried to articulate and use them to better your life in a positive way...or maybe you won't. Maybe you'll forget everything and just move on to another book that's some garbage Kardashian-type entertainment bullshit, and that's okay too. After all, you're a little nugget in this universe just like me, and we're all fucked up in our own ways. But, many of us are good in our own ways, too. It just depends on how much of which we want to show most of the time. So, carry on living your cynical and self-indulgent life. Just know that I wish you all the best! Oh, and by the way, I was kidding when I said you might forget this book, because I KNOW you ain't ever gonna forget this shit!

Nina, out!

www.ingramcontent.com/pod-product-compliance
Lightning Source LLC
Chambersburg PA
CBHW050631160426
43194CB00010B/1632